JEAN-PAUL SARTRE

JEAN-PAUL SARTRE

The Method and Aspiration of his Philosophy

Arnabi Sen

KALPAZ

Jean-Paul Sartre : The Method and Aspiration of his Philosophy

ISBN : 978-81-7835-922-9

Published in 2012 in India by
Kalpaz Publications
C-30, Satyawati Nagar,
Delhi - 110052
E-mail: kalpaz@hotmail.com
Ph.: 9212729499

Laser Type Setting : Rajender Vashist, Delhi
Printed at : Chawla Offset Printers, Delhi

Contents

Contents

Preface

This work has been undertaken, to point out, the age old idea about Sartre's philosophy that it followed the phenomenological method and it, lacks evidential support. Sartre himself criticised the phenomenology as an 'escapist doctrine' as it 'brackets' out existential world for transcendental analysis. Sartre's philosophy has preferred to go through every profile of existential world. No attempt has been made by the commentators of Sartre's philosophy so far to differentiate the method of Sartre's philosophy from that of phenomenology, which has been done in this work. Philosophical work of Sartre is also differentiated from that of Heidegger. To find out the historical moorings of Sartre's philosophical method, his philosophy is compared with and differentiated from Hermeneutic Philosophy.

Through the effort of tracing out Sartre's philosophical method, his thoughts are analysed and clarified in this work. This clarification has made Sartre's philosophical jargon easier to understand. The semblance of Sartre's philosophy as individualistic can also be removed in its deeper analysis by clarifying his effort to reconcile between subjectivity or between individuality and totality.

In this work the thought of different philosophers such as Husserl, Heidegger and Hermeneutic are tried to be simplified as far as possible. This will help students initially, to get into the thought of these stalwarts.

The work is enriched with the invaluable suggestions of Dr. Asha Mukherjee of Visva Bharti, Dr. Goutam Biswas of Gauhati University and Renowned Specialist of Sartre's Philosophy in India, Dr. Mrinal Kanti Bhadra, whose work on Sartre has also been discussed in this thesis.

Arnabi Sen

Preface

Introduction

Sartre is an representative authority on atheist philosophy of the twentieth century, is an outstanding creation and contribution to the world of philosophy and literature immense. The twentieth century which was in the want of a rigorous doctrine to show man a direction in his life, came as an attack against all conventions and systems. Awareness was brought about in man about his solitude and responsibility by many authors such as Camus, Graham Green, Sartre etc. But Sartre was the lone writer among them who treated the problem of man's life philosophically. His formulation was in philosophical language. He introduced some new coinages which are not unintelligible to the reader. Consciousness as 'for-itself' and being 'in-itself' express most aptly the vacuity of consciousness and opacity of the world to consciousness respectively.

We should mention that Sartre was the lone writer of his time who granted man a total alienation from either the world or himself. Camus, on the other hand, tried to uphold the brotherhood in the people of the world. Sartre made man also the lone medium of the revelation of the world or totality. The world revealed by man is limited to his subjectivity. But human consciousness, at the same time is a non-being which is nothing in itself except a revelation of the world as this or that.

Sartre's later writings were influenced by the economic crisis, fascism, discrimination, deprivation, torture, violence etc. of the post-war situation. He tried to focus on the hurdles of the man's life which are there for ever in the world. At the same time, he upholds the quest of man for the meaning of his freedom which appears as a burden on him. But we should mention that Sartre has contributed a lot to moral philosophy by considering freedom as a reflected power of man. Sartre does not believe in 'reflection' which means to know one's own inside, he does not believe in the existence of any thing inside man but believes in a drive in man to the world. The reflection in Sartrean sense can know or acknowledge man's power to rise above the situation in which man finds himself. We can expect, therefore, with the knowledge of Sartre's philosophy, knows that than his own responsibility in his failures as well as in success. Though the world appears to be an 'objectification' of man, but it is his subjectivity, that along with 'Other's' subjectivity, that is making this world.

The thesis, entitled **Jean-Paul Sartre : The Method and Aspiration of his Philosophy** aims to interpret Sartre's method of philosophising in relation to his concept of man's aspiration. Human aspiration, as discussed by Sartre, remains the focal point of the thesis in bringing out his philosophical method. Emphasis on human aspiration seems to distinguish Sartre's philosophy from that of other philosophers. The initial concept of non-being which he considers about consciousness is due to the aspiration of man. Before Sartre we find Plato, Descartes etc. considering consciousness as a place of idea or thought, so the world of particulars or things remains outside the consciousness. But in Sartre's philosophy consciousness as nothing in-itself exists as a consciousness of the world in order to have something. In Sartre's words it is a "desire to be" being treated as identical to the world, as objectivity, ungraspable by consciousness in its entirety. Consciousness of man is a ceaseless effort of, acquiring all human possibilities in the world.

In all his books, Sartre deals with human aspiration. Although the particular term 'aspiration' is used by him perhaps only once, at the concluding part of ***Being and Nothingness***, to indicate the ultimate desire of man. The ultimate desire, to be the causa-sui, to be the cause of man's own being which is always in action. But in comparison to this desire, other concrete desires such as desire to be a doctor or a politician etc. are not subordinate to it. Rather, it is fundamental to all desires, which makes human desire an infinite process since the end is ungraspable in finite time. In most of Sartre's philosophical books we find him dealing with this fundamental concept of desire. Either he deals with the desire to change the world which is ungraspable and vast or with the concrete desires such as desire for being a doctor or pilot, desire to overcome poverty, desire for having a caring world etc.

We also find Sartre dealing with the concepts such as freedom, responsibility, nothingness, etc. or man's being-for-others, history as totality, world as a totality and their relation to individual man etc. and find everything to indicate man's ceaseless going out of himself towards the world of others, where others are equally going out of themselves and for all this ceaseless going, the only thing which is at the centre, is man's aspiration. If Sartre's philosophy is depicted as either ontology, or epistemology or metaphysics, from all possible angles, man will be seen in Sartre's philosophy, to labour till death. It is for man's own unbound desire or aspiration, man is bound to ceaseless action and ceaseless running after the world. Man's aspirations supersede man's needs, his specific character or identity, and thereby negate the possibility of considering essence in man. Man's endless aspiration makes his freedom a burden on him and binds him with action throughout his life.

By considering human aspiration as the focal point we can cover all the philosophical and literary works of Sartre and also bring out his philosophical method. Man who is found with his particular desires can have the maximum possibility to aspire a being equal to God which does not suggest any end or essence of desire but an endlessness or infinity itself.

Sartre's philosophical method appears to be an outstanding one as compared to the phenomenological method of Husserl and Heidegger. Like Husserl, Sartre does not 'bracket' existential world, or like Heidegger he does not posit 'Being' before consciousness or before human reality. Being and consciousness are 'contemporaneous' for Sartre. The outstanding feature of Sartre's philosophical method consists in his description of consciousness as 'nothing' in itself which exists as a consciousness of the world. But the 'being' or the characteristics of the world which is not 'nothing' in itself but indicates a totality, is forever separated from the consciousness. Consciousness characterises man who has neither a being nor a definition. In order to have a being and definition man is directed towards the world. And we cannot think of a world without consciousness which knows it. The world is revealed by consciousness as this or that or in profiles, infinitely. Thus Sartre does not believe in an essential knowledge of the world or in a transcendental consciousness either rather he believes in an infinite process of knowing the world by the consciousness. Thus consciousness characterises man's effort, to have a definition, also as an infinite process. So man is reduced to action. Man's 'freedom' indicates his freedom to act but no freedom not to act. Thus man becomes responsible for his action without being responsible for his reducibility to action. Naturally, man wants to be responsible for his being which is reduced to action, he wants to be the cause of himself. He tries to have a primacy over his being. But it is not possible, since it may put an end to his infinite reducibility to action.

The 'Being', which man aspires to be, indicates the meaningfulness of man's constant going beyond his present situation. Man does not want to have a being like a book or a pen. The 'being' which man aspires is not devoid of the possibility of action. Man wants to act according to his wishes and not under any compulsion. This 'Being' is not reduced to action, but has the possibility of action according to his wish, is the cause of his own action, is identical only with the traditional concept of God. Sartre holds, therefore, that man wants to be God means man wants to have freedom instead of being reduced to it.

It seems that human aspiration is a mixture of both 'bad faith' and 'good 'faith' – the two unique concepts upheld by Sartre to describe man's attitude towards himself. Man's aspiration is partly an expression of 'good faith' since he tries to overcome his reducibility to action and wants to be a complete 'being'. But he is in 'bad faith' when he is denying that he has freedom and trying to posses freedom. When man's aspiration goes through worshipping God, he is expressing simply 'bad faith' because he is denying his freedom and wants to be at the mercy of God for the consequences he faces in his life. Actually he himself with others is responsible for the consequences he faces. On the other hand, by aspiring to be God, man is not denying his responsibility. But by aspiring to be responsible for his being that is by aspiring to be the cause of his being, he is aspiring to have a control over his ceaseless action. This control or primacy seems to be considered by Sartre as an obstruction to the continuous flow of man's action and would transform man into an object.

The thesis, therefore, has its *first chapter on Sartre's Ontology of Man as a desire to be.* In this chapter the 'being' which is desired, is characterised after Sartre's exposition in *Being and Nothingness, Psychology of Imagination* and *Emotion*. Sartre describes man as desire to be and this 'desire' indicates a 'lack' in man. Man lacks 'being' which he desires, but for Sartre this being is not identical with the being of the object which indicates inaction, rather a 'primacy' over the being of man which has possibility of action. The infinite possibility of the action of man reveals the being as ungraspable.

In *Psychology of Imagination* and *Emotion,* we find that primarily man aspires to change the empirical world. Since, man finds the world 'too difficult' for everything in it, is infinitely related with something else and the pursuit of man to know the world gets neither a rest nor any support. Thus man's aspiration is rooted in his being thrown into the empirical world. Man finds 'lack' in the empirical world which is actually brought by man as he is marked by infinitely unfulfilled desire. When he finds all the roads of the world are blocked that goes towards his fulfillment, he imagines an absent world which is complete which indicates the fulfillment of his aspiration too. Thus he can get a complete being which is not simply reduced to run after the profiles of the world but it is at the apex of his own running.

In *chapter 2* we try to bring out *Sartre's Method to Reach the Idea of 'Being',* from the perspective of empirical knowledge. First, we have tried to bring out the outstanding features of Sartre's philosophical method. In this context a comparison is made between the method of Sartre and that of Husserl and

Heidegger. It seems that Sartre can reconcile between the subjective method of Husserl and objective method of Heidegger. Husserl considers ontology to centre around the "essential cognition" of the world by the consciousness. On the other hand, for Heidegger, Being is there in the world which is a self revealing being, illuminates man as a being in the world or Being. Second, it is explained in this chapter, how Sartre has considered the 'form of being' which is the 'essence of being' in Husserlian term, cannot be grasped through perception, in its 'entirety' because perception is always in profiles. Sartre does not believe that through empirical observation of the particular aspects, the 'form of the object can be induced. For Sartre when man finds the world to be too difficult to grasp in its entirety, he can imagine an 'absent' world of entirety. But as our imagination takes its elements from the world of perception we tried to see whether imagination has any similarity with process of induction. The apparent similarity does not remain of course in the deeper analysis of Sartre's method.

For Sartre, man's 'fundamental project' that is the aspiration 'to be God' of one's own, is expressed in man's all particular projects. He does not find any need of deriving 'fundamental project' from particular projects. But it is true that there is no explicit projection by us for being God, it has to be intuited. The project that is not explicit cannot be judged empirically or experientially. He accepts 'a priori description' as a method to intuit 'fundamental project'. But if Sartre's method is an a priori description, then Sartre's method is not compatible with his rejection of Husserl's method of "phenomenological reduction". In Husserl's method "Transcendental ego" is conceived as a "universal evidence" for the essential knowledge of the world as he rejects the scientific knowledge of the world as a source of perplexity. For this, he brackets existential world and believes in the phenomenological experience by consciousness. But Sartre finds consciousness to be directed towards the 'evanescent' world infinitely without grasping it in its entirety at a time that is without having an essential knowledge of it. It brings 'anguish' in consciousness. Sartre finds an escapist attitude in bracketing the existential world by "phenomenological reduction", an escape from the anguish of consciousness is noticed thereby.

Sartre seems to reconcile between subjective and objective stand, point which can be taken on human reality. Induction with which we can trace some similarity in his concept of imagination of an absent world cannot be the method of Sartre for his description of human aspiration because induction is an objective method of understanding since it is based on empirical observation of particular events. There is no scope in induction to observe man's emotional drive towards the empirical world. Man's perception of the world in profiles can be interpreted through empirical observation. But to interpret the surpassing of the world by man in order to imagine a changed or 'not yet' world, there should be a subjective stand point taken on human reality. An 'a priori description' can very well reconcile between subjective and objective stand, 'point'. But we cannot dissociate Sartre's method from experience and it was not intended by him either. We tried to bring out an experiential stand-point.

In continuation of our previous chapter, we have tried to discuss Sartre's concept of 'human aspiration on the basis of 'particular project' in *chapter 3*. The 'particular project' for Sartre, designs the 'global project' which indicates the "universal human purpose". But the 'particular project' are not determined by the 'global project' because the 'global project' itself remains undetermined due to the freedom of the 'particular project' of man. Sartre believes in a "universal human purpose". We tried to interpret Sartre's concept of human aspiration through inductive inference since it seems that Sartre derives the "universal human purpose" from the 'particular project' of man. Sartre believes that the "universal purpose" is expressed in every 'particular project' and there is no need to prove it, which is needed in an inductive inference. So, here once again we deal with Sartre's purpose to reconcile between subjective purpose and objective purpose of man.

Moreover, Sartre claims that human aspiration develops in 'Spiral'. Sartre finds to give rise to single fundamental desire of being the 'foundation' of man's own being, all 'particular' desires. Man's every 'particular project' rises up from the 'fundamental project' that is to be the 'foundation' of man's own being. It moves in a circular motion because it expresses the totality of man's aspiration and turns back to individuality to occur again. Every individual action expresses the totality of human aspiration and at the same time to prevent being lost in the totality, turns back to individuality. Thus it tends to form a circle, but due to perpetual individual action, it can never complete the circle but form a spiral. This 'spiral' cannot be interpreted through the inductive inference. It seems that the inductive inference is a linear method which goes from particular to universal. Sartre's method should reconcile between particular and universal as well as subjective and objective. We find an analogy between particular and subjective and between universal and objective because in Sartre's interpretation we note that the "universal" does not indicate the generality of 'particular projects'. But it seems that 'particular project' being viewed not from subjective angle but from a global angle, is considered as "universal human purpose" where subjectivity is lost. Such reconciliation is livelier when Sartre interprets man in a "social-historical world". Such interpretation which reconciles between subjective and objective stand-points taken on human reality through the mediation of history is similar to the hermeneutical interpretation.

In *chapter 4* of the thesis we discuss the concept of history or 'life world' of the hermeneutic philosophers such as Dilthey, Recoeur, Habermas and Gadamar. As historically viewed, hermeneutics can loosely be defined as the theory of interpretation of a text by clearing complexity that is by tracing back the historical and cultural background of author's writings. The text considered to be the representation of particular age. Some similarity between Sartrean and hermeneutical stand-point is discussed here so as to show how Sartre is interpreting the complexity of human behaviour as a representation of historical background. In this chapter we are primarily concerned with the concept of hermeneutics which offers a theory of historical understanding. It is through Droysen's writing, understanding got a technical meaning in the twentieth century. He does not believe in an objective history and for him past is 'inaccessible', at the same time historian can understand history as he himself is affected by the events of the past. Consequently, hermeneutical understanding of history can concern itself with both subjective and objective condition of understanding. Droysen believes history to be an expression of man's inner nature. The historian would not find historical events alien to him. He believes in a process of understanding history in which 'part' is understood within the framework of the 'whole' from which it was originated. The 'whole' is understood only from the perspective of the 'part' in which it finds an expression. This is the main Droysenian framework in which we will proceed to discuss the concepts of Dilthey, Ricoeur, Habermas, Gadamar by comparing them with Sartre's concept of History. In Sartre's philosophy, subjectivity is considered as the sole expression of the whole the human history.

History for Dilthey seems to be the "preserved memory" of the "past humanity" which provides 'power' to 'modern men'. From 'lived experience' or past we know the force of an action. In Ricoeur we find history to be conceived as a tool to justify the value of a "present man". Habermas's 'life world' is both the 'context' and the 'possibility' of human action. He made a futuristic interpretation of 'life world' since he finds it as 'recognition' and 'complements' of human action. Gadamar is Hegelian in his approach but has a different contention. He tries to reconcile between subjectivity and objectivity in the understanding of history. Gadamar seems to develop "historical understanding" as a requirement of consciousness to have an essential knowledge of human reality. Consciousness should develop the "horizon" of thinking by bringing out a 'fusion' between the present and the past. It can do this, according to Gadamar, by considering history as a 'testimony' for man's present 'hope' and 'fear'. Present man seems to represent the subjective side of the human reality whereas history as a preserved memory, as power or testimony, represents the objective side of the human reality but actually it is constructed through subjectivity. But there is some difference between Sartre's consideration of history and that others, which we have discussed in this chapter. According to sertrs is neither a "preserved memory" nor a 'value' nor a 'testimony' of man's present action. According to Sartre, like Habermas History is both past and future for Sartre but not complements or recognition but 'objectification'. History is devoid of subjectivity as it is made up of "men in plural", it surpasses the expectation of single man and objectifies him.

In *Chapter 5,* we have tried to bring out a hermeneutical stand-point in Sartre's philosophising. Here, we concentrate on his interpretation of man in a "social-historical" context. It is "social-historical" world which appears as 'possibility' for some individual or community, but at the same time appears as impossibility for some other individual or community. Study of medicine, for example, is a social possibility but impossibility to those who cannot afford to study it. Thus even at the presence of social possibility man may find 'lack' in himself. Being a crew member is another possibility may appear as impossibility for those who are prohibited from being a crew member. All the possibilities in the social, historical world which are not yet achieved by man indicate 'lack' in man. Even most privileged group of a society finds 'lack' in themselves and eager to get one after another. The problem is that the socio-historical world has enormous possibility which is not acquired by individual since the socio-historical world is made up of 'Other', not by any one man but by the "men in plural". The consciousness of 'lack' drives man towards the world to surpass it. The man who is prohibited from being a 'crew member' is prohibited by the socio-historical world of 'Other'. He tries to surpass it by stealing a plane by flying it over to France. But at the same time, he is creating history when he as an "air plane thief" was killed in France and it provoked a revolt in "black community" against English caste system. Thus the social-historical world objectifies man which is also made by man. With unfulfilled expectation, man tries to surpass the objective world in order to save his subjectivity. The history of mankind thus works as a provocation for man's action as well as objectification of him as his subjectivity is lost in it.

In this way, Sartre, through the mediation of history, shows how 'nothingness' comes into the world. 'Nothingness' is both the feeling of 'lack' in man and the drive of man to surpass it. The idea of Sartre is interpreted here as to have a socio-historical moorings, with an emphasis on the hermeneutical effort of Sartre's philosophising to reconcile between subjectivity and objectivity. Sartre considers socio-historical world to be an 'objectivity' or 'impossibility' by explicating man's experience of a world which surpass him.

We conclude the discussion by pointing out Sartre's method of philosophising as an experiential-intuitive one. Right from the concept of consciousness to objectification of man, Sartre's philosophy appears to be an experiential interpretation of man's life. The explication of consciousness as the consciousness of the world and the separate existence of it forever from the consciousness seems to be the out come of the experience of man's alienation from himself as well as from the outside world. Everything which I have to acquire for me is there in the outside world. The world is intuitively known as a source of my objectification as I find my subjectivity lost in. Such experience became strong in men in post war situation of the world. So we have tried to point out this special situational experiential tone of Sartre's philosophy.

1

Sartre's Ontology of Man as a Desire to be

Sartre's phenomenological ontology can be defined as the ontology of man. Human consciousness and its dialectical relation to the world and other men is the content of his ontology. As an existentialist, Sartre in his opposition to essentialism and reductionism holds that being of man can neither be inferred from a given essence nor be reduced to a substance respectively. Sartre's discussion of man starts with the difference which he made between consciousness and 'being'. He differentiates them in terms of having a 'self' and not having a 'self'. Consciousness is a "pure appearance" for Sartre, which exists as a consciousness of object. Consciousness has nothing in itself. Consciousness is "what it is not". Contrarily, object is "What it is". The difference characterises the difference between man and the world in Sartre's philosophy. World indicates a 'being' whereas man being characterised as consciousness of the world is 'nothing' in itself and directed towards the world as a *desire to be*. Consciousness is 'for-itself' whereas object is 'in-itself'. Man's desire is directed towards the empirical world of 'things' and 'quality' but Sartre does not say that man wants to be the world or things.

Desire Signifies a Lack

We shall try to discuss what does 'being' mean which man aspires for. Human reality lacks 'being' of its own.

> Consciousness— does not coincide with itself in a full equivalence.[1]

> The existence of desire as a human fact is sufficient to prove that human reality is lack.[2]

The question arises how desires such as thirst, hunger etc. can prove human reality to be 'lack'? Sartre answers such question by pointing out that the desire belongs to human being who finds 'lack' in himself. A "half cycle" is lacking but cannot desire to be complete since the circle is neither half nor full to itself. It is consciousness which finds the circle half. For Sartre, it is the felt requirement of the other that half causes the "half circle" to be considered as half. But if man finds lack in himself, it is not because he knows the totality or essence of himself. We should notice in this regard that though Sartre supports Husserl's notion of 'intentionality' of consciousness that it has no inside but he does not support his notion of "transcendental ego" as an "apodictic evidence" of the essential knowledge of the world. Husserl 'brackets the existential' world by considering it as a source of perplexity for its unending series of revelation. Sartre does not believe that consciousness can be support of essential knowledge. Rather, consciousness is totally an outward drive towards the existential world and does not know its essential nature throughout its existence. It does not know due to the unending series of appearance of the world and due to the very being of consciousness which cannot remain in any static situation but goes out of itself and remains as a lack.[3]

> ...human reality is not something which exists first in order afterwards to lack this or that: it exists first as lack and in immediate synthetic connection with what it lacks

It seems that for Sartre man exist as 'lack' and directed towards that which he lacks out-side of himself. Thus human reality is always directed towards the world. This is called the 'intentionality' of consciousness and here Sartre's concept of 'desire' seems to indicate a psychological requisite for the 'intentional' act of consciousness. In this way desire of water etc. can prove man's 'intentionality' as well as his being as 'lack'. But "desire" proves human reality as 'lack' does not mean that human reality lacks this or that. Rather, Sartre seems to follow Stendhal or Proust's idea of "love" "jealousy" etc. as desires which are aimed at something more than the desired object. Sartre says that it is for "laying hold of the world in its entirety"[4]. So Sartre says for man ... it lacks something for something else.[5] We lack money not for money only but for something else.

The question arises why our desire goes beyond the desired object. Sartre holds that it is not the case that things are 'expelled' from consciousness and it goes towards things; rather consciousness surpasses things since it does not want to be a thing 'in-itself', thus it sustains 'nihilation'.

> The for-itself cannot sustain nihilation without determining itself as a *lack of being*...nihilation does not coincide with a single introduction of emptiness into consciousness. An external being has not expelled the in-itself from consciousness; rather for-itself is perpetually determining itself as not to be the in-itself[6].

The lack which consciousness tries to surpass is a self created lack.

Man Aspires to be God

Being as in-itself is not the end of man who is a desire to be. But as he is a constant surpassing of that which is 'in-itself', the 'end' for which man aspires, must be of a complex nature. The end posited by consciousness cannot be the being in a static sense.

> ...consciousness – wishes to have the impermeability and an infinite destiny of the in-itself.[7]

The question arises how can there be an "infinite destiny" of in-itself? To answer this question Sartre says:

> ...human reality is the desire of being in-itself. But the in-itself which it desires cannot be the pure contingent absurd in-itself comparable at every point to that which it encounters and which it nihilates...Quite the contrary, what the for-itself demands of the in-itself is precisely the totality detotalised – "in-itself is nihilated in for-itself" — The fundamental value which presides over this project is exactly the in-itself-for-itself : that is, ideal of consciousness which would be the foundation of its own being-in-itself.... It is this ideal which can be called God.[8]

The unification of the 'in-itself' and 'for-itself' as the 'foundation' of the "being-in-itself" seems to indicate a primacy of the consciousness over the 'facticity' of the 'for-itself'. The 'facticity' of it, is its "presence to the world". It is his given being so can be conceived as his 'being in-itself'. Man finds himself as being thrown into the world and as being directed towards the things towards the 'in-itself'.

> The for-itself is, in so far as it appears in condition which it has not chosen, as Pierre is a French bourgeois in 1942. Schmitt was a Berlin worker in 1870: it is in so far as it is thrown into and abandoned in a "situation": It is as pure contingency inasmuch as for it as for things in the world, as for this wall, this tree, this cup. It is in so far as there is in it something of which he is not the foundation – its presence to the world.[9]

Man finds himself in this world in a particular condition which he has not chosen, for example, his nation, the time of his birth, the socio-political condition etc. All these indicate his thrownness in the world since these are all given to him, not chosen by him. These conditions are his faticity which are permanently with him. But Sartre believes that every human action is to surpass the 'being' which is given to him. Their surpassing can also be considered as a part of man's facticity. Man's drive towards the world is also given to him. In order to surpass the given reality of the drive man wants to be the foundation of his drive. This 'nihilating' act brings 'nothingness' into the world. Thus man becomes the 'foundation' of his 'lack'.

> ...Nothingness – comes to being through a particular being, which is human reality....human reality is being in so far as within its being and for its being it is the unique foundations of nothingness at the heart of being.[10]

Thus, Sartre shows how man as the "foundation" of his own 'nothingness' wants to be the 'foundation' of "own being in-itself" the being of him which is always a presence to the world and surpassing the world. Sartre has made it clear that the world or the "in-itself" cannot be the 'foundation'.

> The in-itself cannot provide the foundation for anything; - it is the foundation of itself in so far as it is *already no longer* in-itself ....But the peculiar possibility of being – is of being the foundation of itself as consciousness through the sacrificial act which nihilates being.[11]

It may appear that the 'in-itself' being revealed by the consciousness cannot be the 'foundation' of consciousness since it is revealed as to be nihilated. But for both Husserl and Sartre the phenomenal world has a perpetually 'evanescent' reality that is a perpetually fading appearance which may be a cause for the 'nihilating' act of consciousness.

> Perpetually evanescent contingency of the in-itself which without ever allowing itself to be apprehended, haunts the for-itself and reattaches it to being-in-itself – this contingency is what we shall call the facticity of the for-itself.[12]

It seems that perhaps the evanescent world is the cause of the nihilation. But to avoid the contradiction which seems to appear here, we should make it clear that the infinite series of the fading appearance of the world is not itself responsible for the nihilation of consciousness rather it has been nihilated by consciousness itself.

> Consciousness is its own foundation but it remains contingent *in order there may be a* consciousness rather than infinity of pure simple in-itself.[13]

The 'totality' for which man aspires is the foundation of man's being and it is not a non-human totality of "in-itself". The word God used by Sartre does not indicate a being beyond human reality. Rather it indicates an aspect of human consciousness which is not yet but for which man aspires.

> ...the being towards which human reality surpasses itself is not a transcended God: it is at the heart of human reality; it is only human reality itself as totality...[14]

Here we can discuss how Sartre seems to differentiate between God which man aspires to be and God to whom man prays. Prayer for Sartre is acceptance by man of his limitations. He takes refuge in God by considering Him to be all powerful. When we pray to God we deny our freedom and our subjectivity.

> Prayer implies *acceptance*. There is an a priori recognition of an operative freedom and its operations. As soon as I no longer agree, I can no longer pray or I pray in bad faith ... it is born from a feeling of total powerlessness – My powerlessness transformed into a negation of my freedom and the feeling of the other's power transformed into a revelation of His pure freedom.[15]

Though the nature of both of God and man aspires to be and to whom he prays are similar, but prayer as a human action is an expression of 'bad faith'. Human aspiration cannot simply be an expression of 'bad faith'. The power which man denies in bad faith of worship is not denied in his aspiration. Human aspiration is an expression of both 'bad faith' and 'good faith'. When man tries to be God, he is denying his freedom', a 'pure freedom' which only God can have. In prayer man does not believe to possess freedom by himself but by God. In human aspiration of pure freedom, pure freedom is not considered as impossible to be achieved but in prayer such possibility is denied.

'Bad faith' is conscious intentional expression of man, a lie to oneself. It is not an ordinary lie which simply the hiding of truth from others. In 'bad faith' man hides truth from himself.

> The ideal description of the liar would be a cynical consciousness, affirming truth within him and denying truth in his words...[16]

> The situation cannot be the same for bad faith. ...is indeed a lie to one-self – thus duality of deceiver and deceived does not exist here.[17]

It seems that human aspiration is an expression of both 'good faith' and 'bad faith'. According to Sartre in 'good faith' man "seeks to flee inner disintegration", Man's inner disintegration consists in his effort of being "what he is not". In good faith man tries to be "what it is"; tries to acquire a self. But in 'bad faith' man tries to flee this disintegration by denying this disintegration.[18] In 'bad faith' man denies that he has no self. Man pretends that he has a self and he tries to flee from it. In human aspiration man tries to acquire a self which is the expression of his 'good faith'; but at the same time he tries to assert his freedom to distance himself from being the 'in-itself', as if he is trying to get rid of the 'self' or "what it is" by denying that he is already a non-self or "what it is not". The nature of human aspiration Sartre would have to accept that it is an expression of both 'good faith' and 'bad faith'.

Faith and Possibility of Aspiration

In relation to the end posited in human aspiration that is to be the God, we can see how man expresses two kinds of faith together. When man wants to be God, he wants to posses all source of objectification within himself and project subjectivity. Here he tries to have a self also. For Sartre, God of human aspiration is a unity of 'in-itself' and for itself. Effort to acquire a self is an expression of good faith but an effort to acquire a 'for-itself. Freedom or subjectivity is the expression of 'bad faith' since he already possesses it. Thus man objectifies himself before other and pretends that he has no subjectivity or freedom to over-come objectification. He aspires to be the master of all objectification, pretends that he is not the master of his objectification.

> ... in prayer I am first of all an object. My nature is to be an object within this freedom. This in no way means I abdicate my freedom, — this freedom becomes one of my objective qualities, one of my properties. I encounter myself in my truth which is to be Being not an existent. What is more I am seen through by Lord's or God's look who knows me as I know myself.[19]

For Sartre in 'bad faith' man does not give up his freedom but denies it. When I allow myself to be beaten, I give up my freedom, it is not a 'bad faith', the 'bad faith' comes in when I deny my responsibility. Similarly, when I pray, I believe in some external power which can make me work. But when man aspires to be God he tries to have a self along with all the power within himself which he pretends to lack but does not actually lack. The Being for which man aspires is a unity of 'in-itself-for-itself'; is a unique 'in-itself' with the possibility of action. It is complete, has no need or compulsion of action. Thus as man aspires to have a self, he gives up freedom, the self he spires is not devoid of subjectivity or freedom. One can say that by aspiring to have an 'operative' or 'pure' freedom which is not reduced to action man is expressing his 'good faith' since he desires a kind of freedom what he actually lacks. The primacy he aspires by becoming God, may also be a sign of 'good faith' since he lacks that primacy. But the primacy to freedom seems to indicate a denial of freedom. So at some point man aspires by denying the 'inner disintegration' or freedom and is expressing bad faith.

Thus in aspiring to be the foundation of being man expresses both 'good faith' and 'bad faith'. As a mixed expression of both of the faith man's aspiration takes the form of an aspiration for the freedom by the freedom. We can say man's aspiration points to a possibility.

> Thus the original relation of for-itself to the self perpetually outlines a project of identification of for-itself with an absent for-itself which it is and what it lacks. What is given as the peculiar lack of each for-itself and what is strictly defined as lacking to precisely this for-itself – is the possibility of the for-itself.[20]

The question arises what kind of 'possibility' is it? From Sartre's discussion it seems that what man is not yet, is his 'possibility'. We find Sartre saying that man lacks 'in-itself'. But 'possibility' does not belong to 'in-itself'. Sartre explains that the "possibility of rains" is not the "possibility of could" it is not even the possibility of 'me' though I perceive the 'possibility'. It is a "concrete reality" for Sartre. Sartre believes that for a 'possibility' to be thought of an 'object' man should be there who is a possibility of himself. We have already pointed out that for Sartre man's 'possibility' does not consist in his possession of the 'self', rather consists in not being the 'self'.

> ...the consciousness of thirst is the consciousness of drinking. We know moreover that coincidence with self is impossible, for the for-itself attained by the

> realisation of the possible will make it-self be as for-itself – that is with another horizon of possibilities.[21]

From the discussion of Sartre it seems that the "horizon of possible" enlarges to that extent in which man goes out of his personal for-itself and enters into a general impersonal 'for-itself'. Man's "horizon of possibility" includes 'Other' too in it. 'God' which man aspires to be, seems to be the 'foundation' of man's being that is directed towards the world that includes 'other'.

> This fundamental desire in turn expresses concretely in the world within the particular situation enveloping the individual, an abstract meaningful structure which is the desire of being in general, it must be considered as human reality in the person, and it brings about its community with others, thus making it possible to state that there is a truth concerning man and not only concerning individuals who cannot be compared. Absolute concreteness, completion, existence as totality belong then to the free and fundamental desire which is the unique person.[22]

Thus man's desire points to a unique person who is in the world but has a control over it, over its people and action. This desire is a human desire, common to all men.

Aspiration and Being for other

Man aspires to a 'Being' in general the explanation of which lies in Sartre's notion of man's 'being-for other'. The static 'in-itself' which man tries to surpass is imposed upon man by 'other' through their look etc. for Sartre. Man passes judgment even on himself as 'shy' or 'proud' being 'objectified' by 'Other'. For this Sartre does not find 'Other' to take any action, their mere presence makes 'me' an 'in-itself'. Every concrete possibility such as my being 'seated' etc. are there due to 'Other'.

> There is however no question of a comparison between what I am for myself and what I am for the other

> as if I found in myself, in the mode of being of the Far-itself, an equivalent of what I am for the Other ... I am unable to bring about any relation between what I am in the intimacy of the For-itself without distance recoil, without perspective and this unjustifiable being in-itself which I am for the Other.[23]

For Sartre man finds himself as an object for 'Other'.

> Genet learns objectively what he is objectively. It is this transition that is going to determine his entire life.[24]

One cannot be shy of any of his gesture unless 'Other' look at him. There is no question of reflecting into one's own consciousness to find him shy. In relation to the refutation of Husserl's concept of 'transcendental ego'[25] , Sartre refutes "reflecting consciousness". Sartre denies that if consciousness is to be reflected upon as shy etc, there has to be a "reflecting consciousness" which would reflect consciousness as shy, proud etc. Sartre then believes, there will be a superimposition of the consciousness which is shy and the consciousness which is reflecting it to be shy. The consciousness which is reflecting appears as not shy. For Sartre, the consciousness which is a "non-reflecting consciousness" or a "pre-reflective consciousness" can be shy, can be proud but cannot reflect itself to be proud. It seems that it can find itself to be proud through the 'looks' of the 'Other'. Thus consciousness of a man becomes an object to himself, not by himself but by 'Others' which Sartre may not agree with.

By refuting the possibility of reflection, Sartre negates the possibility of consciousness for being the object for itself without being objectified by 'Other'. Man always finds himself as engaged in certain action as directed towards out-side.

> ... I cannot truly define myself as being in a situation, - because I am my own nothingness. In this sense – and since I am not what I am – I cannot even define myself as *truly being* in the process of listening at the door.[26]

When a man is involved in 'eves dropping' he is totally engrossed in his action. He cannot judge himself to be listening at door but can only listen at the door.

> ... my possibilities are present to my unreflective consciousness in so far as the 'Other' is watching me.[27]

> Caught in the act, someone has entered and watching him. Beneath his gaze, the child comes to himself. He who was not yet anyone, suddenly becomes Jean Genet. He feels that he is blinding, deafening; he beacons an alarm is singing.[28]

Genet, the child thief, was, simply an action without being looked at by someone else. But the moment he was watched by somebody, he became a thief to himself.

> A voice declares publicly; you are a thief – Genet, thunderstruck, considers his act, looks at him from every angle. No doubt about it, it is theft.[29]

Sartre makes it clear that the objectification or being proud or shy in the eyes of other is by subject's choice. In pride or shame man is not passive. Rather man chooses him to be proud or shy, but for others. We could find a very interesting remark by Sartre in this context.

> Pride could never be satisfied by a form of originality which had been passively accepted and of which he himself was not the author.[30]

Thus in man's objectification by other, man's freedom is kept intact.

In the same way, the existence of 'Other', is revealed to me. 'Other' is revealed to me as a source of 'objectivity' and 'alienation'. But as man's being and man's aim both consist in being "What it is not" or consist in surpassing "What it is", man always tries to surpass the 'objectivity' imposed upon him by 'Other', so he tries to impose 'objectivity' on 'Other'.

> ... Other existence was experienced with evidence in and through the fact of my objectivity – my reaction to my own alienation for the 'other' was expressed in my grasping the other as an object.[31]

Now we could make out in what way man's "being-for-other" is related to our desire. For Sartre, our "being-for-other", limits our 'freedom', our 'subjectivity'. This limitation is chosen by ourselves only. Man follows the direction such as "train timings, "notices" etc. furnished by others. We follow these just to choose our way of being, we find these techniques acceptable for our purpose.

> We must recognise that – a real limit to our freedom – that is a way of being which is imposed on us without our freedom being its foundation. Still it is necessary to understand this; the limit imposed does not come from the action of others – even torture does not dispose us from our freedom; when we give in, we do so freely.[32]

Sartre seems to believe in a "human situation" for which "other need not act directly on man but mere presence and action of other makes human situation which is chosen by man and indicates man's objectivity". It seems that we limit our freedom by our freedom.

> We are not lumps of clay, and what is important is not what people make of us but what we ourselves make what they make of us. It is like a return to the individual state of man if and when individual accepts general situation.[33]

> Thus the very meaning of our free choice is to cause a situation to arise which expresses this choice, a situation, the essential characteristics of it is to be *alienated*; that is to exist as a form of in-itself for the other. Therefore, we have to do with an essential characteristic of all situations in general; this characteristic can not act upon its content, but it is

> accepted and recovered by the same being who puts himself into a situation. We can not escape this alienation since it would be absurd even to think of existing otherwise than a situation.[34]

Thus it seems that for Sartre, man exists in a 'situation' which is a general ground of objectification" of both myself and 'Other'. Even Sartre holds that my identification as professor, waiter, ugly, beautiful etc. are realised on the perspective of this "general ground". As we find Genet to make himself on the basis of such a ground. Genet once said, "I decided to be what crime made me"[35]. But Sartre has made it clear that the terms used for the identification are not used in the same sense in which 'Others' use it for me. Sartre calls them unrealisable.

> ... This unrealisable; it is in fact my limit – it cannot exist as the limit of a given being but only as the limit of my freedom. This means that my freedom by freely choosing itself chooses its limits, or, if you prefer the free choice of my ends.[36]

We have discussed how consciousness finds itself thrown into the world and as a ceaseless drive towards the things of the world as a 'desire'. Apart from this drive it has nothing within itself. So it aims to have a 'self', this does not mean that it tries to be an 'in-itself'. Rather it surpasses the 'in-itself'. For Sartre consciousness tries to get a 'self' which is a totality of 'in-itself' and 'for-itself'. The self which man aspires is not devoid of the 'possibility' like the self of the 'in-itself'. Man is thrown into the world of things and 'Other'. Thus man is 'being-for-other' in this being man is 'identified' as well as 'objectified'. He surpasses it by objectifying 'Other'. Thus consciousness finds itself in a 'general' 'situation' of objectification or 'alienation' along with 'Other'. For this objectification there is no need of any deliberate action of 'Other'. Rather the 'objectification' of me by 'Other' or the 'objectification' of 'Other' by me is the expression of my 'freedom' only. If it is considered as 'limitation' by Sartre, it is so considered since I am not the 'foundation' of my 'freedom'. Man tries to be the 'foundation' of his being. He tries to be at the onset of everything that happens to him he tries to use his freedom as a 'tool' which he cannot.

> Freedom is neither given nor a property it can only be by choosing itself. The freedom of for-itself is always *engaged*; there is no question here of a freedom – which could pre-exist its choice.[37]

We find Sartre discussing that man does not want to be a freedom identified with action. He wants freedom as a property. But property belongs to 'in-itself', man has no property or anything inside it, what he has is only a drive. He wanted to be something whose very nature was a contradiction he wanted to be a freedom thing.[38]

> He chooses to exist for himself as he was for others. He wanted his freedom to appear to himself like a 'nature', he wanted this nature which other discovered in him to appear to them like the very emanation of his freedom.[39]

This tendency of man appears as a self objectification, it is significant for the destiny of man. The manner in which man projects his freedom is related to his destiny.

> The free choice which man makes of himself is completely identified with that which is called his destiny.[40]

Thus it seems that if Sartre holds that man wants to be God, man's ceaseless effort to assert his freedom want to be supported by a 'Being' which enjoys freedom, and performs action according to his wish. Thus consequently, he finds the ultimate desire of man as comparable to God. Sartre does not say that man's desires are constituted by the end of being 'God'. It seems that man's desire which goes as an unending process and which includes all men of the world in an encountering manner, can be meaningful only by conceiving an end as God which is all pervasive and has a control over all actions of all individuals.

> It may be asked if man on coming into the world is borne towards God as towards his limit, if he can choose only to be God, what becomes of freedom? For freedom is nothing other than a choice which creates for itself its own possibilities, but it appears here that the initial project of becoming God which "defines" man comes close to being the same as a human "nature" or an essence. The answer is that while the meaning of the desire is ultimately the project of being God, the desire is never constituted by this meaning; on the contrary, it always represents a particular discovery of its ends. These ends are in fact pursued in terms of particular empirical situation...[41]

Here we could note T.C. Anderson's remarks on Sartre. Anderson finds Sartre to uphold an abstract concept of freedom, in his earlier writings, as absolute freedom, without considering its limits. But in his later writing he concentrates more on the actual possibility of freedom. He considers economic and technological limits that determine human action. In the concluding remark of Being and Nothingness, Anderson finds Sartre to reject God as fundamental project in order to restore an ethical atmosphere in the world.[42] But as we have already discussed that to ensure a freedom without limitation, Sartre does not consider 'becoming God' to be the determinant factor for individual human project. Becoming God indicates for Sartre a 'limit' of man which inhibits freedom. God seems to be the imagined end in order to furnish a reason behind enormous exercise of human freedom. Rather for Sartre all human drives are brute facts of freedom. Anderson finds Sartre rejecting the project as he ignores sympathetic human relation first and accepts later, God in the concluding remark of *Being and Nothingness*. Actually it is not a rejection of God as a project of human action. In Sartre's philosophy, we must notice that

Sartre in his earlier works talked about a "general situation" shared by men, which does not indicate that he did not consider any sympathetic relation among men. Rather considered sympathy as an expression of prudence in premonition of being objectified by others. Second, Sartre expressed doubt in the unlimited freedom, if there is an effort to be God, as the sole project before men. Sartre made it clear that in no way man's actions are controlled by this project. In the concluding remarks of Being and Nothingness Sartre considers "God project as à "determining Value" of human freedom. The value is 'lack' in relation to man. He lacks it. The value itself indicates an ideal presence as a unity of all choices of all men. But in relation to a single man this value is a 'lack'. Man in exercising his freedom, cannot reject this value. This God-project as a "determining value", determines human action in order to be 'what it-is-not' for-ever. Sartre makes it clear that how does human value originate. From Sartre's discussion it seems that human value originates from human action only which aims to be 'what-it-is-not'. The value of causa-sui or God remains a 'lack' in relation to human action forever. Thus it is an ideal value for itself in being 'what-it-is-not'.

> "Ontology has revealed to us, in fact, the origin and the nature of value; we have seen the value is lack in relation to which for-itself determines its being as a lack.
>
> —Man makes himself man in order to be God, and selfness considered from this point of view can appear to be an egoism; but precisely because there is no common measure between human reality and the self cause which it wants to be, one could just as well say that man looses himself in order that self cause may exist.[43]
>
> ... possible could be chosen and rejected *ad libitum*, the theme which made the unity of all choices of possible was the value or ideal presence of the *ens*

> *causa sui* What will become of freedom, If it turns its back upon this value? … is it possible for freedom to take itself as the source of all value, or must it necessarily be defined in relation to transcendent value which haunts it? A freedom which wills itself freedom is in fact, a being-which-is not-what-it-is and which-is-what it-is-not, and which chooses as the ideal of being, being what-it is not and not-being-what-it is.
>
> This freedom chooses then not to recover itself, not to coincide with itself but to be always at a distance from itself.[44]

We have already discussed the possibility of God project as a limit to man's freedom. But freedom cannot also choose to be freedom only or what it is. Freedom implies an action in order for being what-it-is-not. Thus freedom cannot aim to recover freedom, it aims for an ideal being what freedom is not. No 'in-itself' is imposed upon freedom through God project as it remains ungraspable throughout the existence which keeps the freedom the act of being the non-being intact. So Anderson's criticism is not fully acceptable in this regard. It is clear that human aspiration is regarded by Sartre, as a failure, we have discussed the possibility of rejecting such aspiration. Now we can discuss the empirical or concrete desires which may have more possibility of being successful.

Desire and the Empirical World

It is clear that human aspiration is regarded by Sartre as a failure. If Sartre is describing man as "desire to be" he describes him as a failure in terms of what he desires.

> … consciousness as the nihilation of being appears therefore, at one stage a progression toward – being a self cause – the progression however stops there as a result of insufficiency in the being of the for-itself.[45]

Now we can discuss the point Sartre made about human aspiration that the end is a "particular discovery in an empirical world". Man's desire seems to be operative in the empirical world, is expressed in his books *Emotion* and *Psychology of imagination.* In *Emotion* he points out how man's desire is directed "to change the empirical world". Consciousness which is a ceaseless directedness towards the world, as a desire, shifts from one object to another object, finds the world to be 'difficult' to grasp it in its entirety, so tries to change the world.

> ... action as a spontaneous unreflective consciousness constitutes a certain existential level in the world... one can understand all those exigencies and tension of the world which surrounds us... This world might be compared to the moving plates of the coin making machines on which the ball-bearings are made to roll: ...This world is *difficult.* This notion of difficulty is not reflective notion which would imply a relationship to me. It is there on the world: it is a quality of the world given in perception.... At present we can conceive what the emotion is. It is a transformation of the world – When the path, traced out become too difficult, or when we see no path, we can no longer live in so urgent and difficult a world —— however we must act so we try to change the world.[46]

Sartre gives importance to the "existential level of the world" which is not "constituted by consciousness". He does not support "phenomenological reduction" of Husserl and he does not believe in "reflective consciousness". He opposes "phenomenological reduction".

> The purifying reflection of phenomenological reduction can perceive the emotion in so far as it constitutes the world in a magical form "I find it hateful *because* I am angry". But – ordinarily we direct upon the emotive consciousness an accessory

> reflection which certainly perceives consciousness as consciousness, but in so far as it is motivated by the object: I am angry; *because* it is hateful. It is on the basis of this reflection the passion will constitute itself.[47]

Thus perception seems to be the only means for consciousness to be related to the world and the emotion arose out of it can be reflected as arose out of the existence of the empirical world. The question arises how the existence of the world causes an emotion "to change the world"? Sartre seems to find this emotion to originate from the perception of the ceaseless series of appearance of the world. In *Psychology of Imagination* he states that perception itself leads consciousness to the infinity of aspects of the world.

> ... *I always perceive more and otherwise* than I see. It is this incontestable fact – which seems to us, constitutes the very structure of perception.[48]

Like Husserl, Sartre too considers an indepth understanding of perception. Husserl's view of perception as depicted by Sartre is as follows:

> "perception is the act by which consciousness puts itself in the presence of a temporal spatial object ... it determines the present object in relation to aspects not now perceived. What is aimed at, is never the invisible aspect of the object but that visible aspect of thing to which the invisible one corresponds – as the upper surface implies the existence of bottom. – it is evidently this intention supply perception with its fullness and richness.[49]

Sartre considers perception as an intentional act of consciousness which would naturally perceive more than the world that is at present before it.

> There is, therefore, in perception the charm of infinity of images: but this can arise only at the cost of the annihilation of perceptual consciousness.[50]

Imagination also posits 'absent' or 'nothingness' as its object since the object it posits in its entirety is not the actual entirety. When there is an 'image' or an object it is opposed to 'perception', it is given to our intuition as 'absent'. The image of 'Peter' is intuition of 'Peter' which is not present "in actually". Posting of that which is 'absent' is to bring 'nothingness' into the world. It takes place not due to the appearance of the object rather due to the surpassing of consciousness of that appearance.

> The apprehension of nothingness could not occur by an immediate unveiling, it develops in and by the free succession of acts of consciousness, the nothingness is the material of surpassing of the world towards the imaginary – It is the appearance of the imaginary before consciousness which permits the grasping of the process of turning world into nothingness....[51]

The question arises what does the "turning of the world into nothingness" mean?

> The person is crushed in the world, run through by real – However, as soon as he apprehends in one way or another – the whole as a situation, he retreats from it towards that in relation to which he is a *lack*.... [52]

Thus it seems that constant engagement of consciousness in the empirical world and "immediate unveiling" of the 'real' being too 'difficult' consciousness tries to posit a world which is "not yet". In portraying the character of 'Baudelaire' we find some interesting comments by Sartre, in order to express the desire of man for a well defined complete world instead of an evanescent world with infinite relationships. Sartre interprets it as town-man's desire. Sartre also intends to interpret it as human desire as a whole.

> As a town's man he loved the geometrical object which was subjected to human rationalisation ... for

> him the *real* water, *real* light and *real* heat which are found in town and which are already the works of art unified by a governing idea – a justified reality.[53]

We should note that the 'real' which man tries to surpass is different from the 'real light' 'real heat' of 'town'. In 'town' the 'real' is an imaginary creation according to the human aspiration. The real which man tries to surpass is the vast ungraspable, unbound real.

We find Sartre's philosophy to be very much concerned with the empirical world and its inexhaustibility by man's perception of it. Man in Sartre's philosophy appears to be an effort to take a leap from the evanescent world. Man perceives this world and conceived a complete and absent world. Dealing with the method of Sartre's philosophy we will see in the next chapter how does he philosophises human aspiration in relation to this empirical world.

References

1. BN., p. 120.
2. BN., p. 136.
3. BN., p. 120.
4. BN., p. 719.
5. BN., p. 146.
6. BN., p. 134.
7. BN., p. 723.
8. BN., pp. 723-24.
9. BN., p. 127.
10. BN., p. 126.
11. BN., p. 130.
12. BN., p. 131.
13. BN., p. 130.
14. BN., p. 139.
15. BN., p. 216.

16. BN., p. 87.
17. BN., p. 89.
18. BN., p. 116.
19. NE., p. 218.
20. BN., p. 147.
21. BN., p. 154.
22. BN., pp. 724-725.
23. BN., p. 302.
24. Saint Genet, pp. 18.
25. *Ibid.,* p. 49.
26. TE., pp. 51-53.
27. BN., p. 348.
28. BN., p. 353.
29. p. 17. Saint Genet.
30. *Ibid,* pp. 17-18.
31. Baudelaire, p. 65.
32. BN., p. 400.
34. Saint Genet, p. 49.
33. BN., p. 672.
36. Saint Genet, p. 49.
37. BN., p. 678.
38. BN., p. 616.
39. Baudelaire, p. 67.
40. *Ibid.,* p. 184.
41. *Ibid.,* p. 184.
42. Anderson T.C., *Sartre's Two Ethics, Open Court Cicago and La Salle,* Illinois 1993, pp. 49-52.
43. BN., pp. 795-96.
44. *Ibid.,* pp. 797-98.
45. *Ibid.,* p. 788.
46. Emotion, pp. 56-58.
47. *Ibid.,* p. 91.

48. PI., p. 138.
49. *Ibid.*, p. 139.
50. *Ibid.*, p. 140.
51. *Ibid.*, pp. 217-218.
52. *Ibid.*, p. 217.
53. *Ibid.*

2

Sartre's Method to Reach the Idea of Being

The primary focus of this chapter is first on the difference between the philosophical method of Sartre and that of Husserl and Heidegger. Second, we have tried to point out the apparent similarity of Sartre's method of inductive inference and its difference from inductive inference in its deeper analysis. In this connection we concentrate on Sartre's method of portraying the human consciousness in terms of a continuous and ceaseless attempt to grasp trans-phenomenal object. Consciousness for Sartre is nothing in itself but a consciousness of external world. The being of the world is not reduced to its finite series of appearance which consciousness can grasp in a finite time. An infinite process is required. This infiniteness of the appearance of the existential world motivates Husserl for "phenomenological reduction" by considering the world as a source of perplexity of knowledge. By the "immanent cognition" of the "transcendental ego, Husserl proposes in favour of 'essential' knowledge of the existential world. This knowledge is transcendental to the world of space and time. Knowledge, based on space-time context, is the source of all 'perplexity' for Husserl. But this view is criticised by Sartre. Before going into Sartre's criticism, we shall discuss Husserl's idea in this regard.

Departure from Husserl and Heidegger

Philosophy for Husserl cannot be a factual science. It cannot establish thought on the basis of factual data. Consequently, the psychologies of philosophy which deals with man's mind on the basis of biology and Anthropology, is rejected by him. Evidences for knowledge which he accepts are neither facts nor what we believe strongly or inclined to believe. Rather which is given in our intuition is "self evident" and it is the "apodictic evidence" for Husserl. Philosophy for Husserl is concerned with the "possibility of cognition". Natural way of thinking about things pertaining to science is the source of the 'perplexity' and contradiction in 'cognition'. For "indubitable cognition" Husserl recommends a method which is called "phenomenological method", the "general doctrine of essence" which can provide a "scientific theory of knowledge" by giving a clear insight of the essence of cognition, as the first step of the phenomenological orientation.[1] Husserl considers 'cogitation', the mental process, as the only "absolute datum" for the cognition to be indubitable. In this connection he uses a pair of concepts for cognition, such as 'immanence' and 'transcendence'. The former belongs to philosophy and the latter belongs to natural science. Cognition which is "self evident" but intends for something outside itself, is "transcendental". Husserl does not find more 'clarity' in scientific theories, than the physical realities. According to Husserl, scientific theories do not provide any extra clarity about colours than what we get through the actual seeing of the colour. All sciences for Husserl are "phenomena of science" and not the "system of valid truth".

In the second level of phenomenological orientation[2], he emphasises on the need of "phenomenological reduction". This "reduction" is motivated by the question how can cognition reach those which are not immanent to it? Husserl believes that it is by "eidetic abstraction" that is by cognising the 'universality' of object. For him consciousness can reach external world and it gives an "objectivity of essence", thus concept of immanence gets a broader meaning. At this level he does not exclude all transcendentally posited things from cognition and excludes the acceptance' of things as 'existent'. Things should be considered as "pure phenomena"; object of "pure seeing". The essence that is grasped in the phenomenological method is the 'meaning' of the "given object".

At the third level of phenomenological orientation[3] Husserl points out that 'meaning' is 'pure phenomena' it is not related to "that which appears". In case of an "enduring sound" immanent cognition" is related to the present and past of the second. There is objectivity in both past phase of the sound. "Immanent cognition" can reflect the temporal phases, for Husserl, that is of a single object. He thinks that object is temporal; it is only consciousness which can constitutes the "self givenness" of the object. Husserl does not accept that the difference in appearance of the same object is caused by the object which appears, rather he believes that it is 'constituted' by mental process such as perception, imagination, memory, prediction etc. Husserl is not suspicious in any way about the existence of the object but for him the object is exhibited only in "immanent cognition" as an enduring one etc. that is in their essence. Thus the object and their appearance constituted by consciousness are inseparable.

Now we can focus on the difference between Husserl and Sartre's "phenomenological method". Here it should be noted that Sartre opposes the idea of immanence' about consciousness. Though in different context, but he uses the phrase "illusion of immanence"[4] to criticise Hume for considering consciousness as a 'place'. For Hume consciousness is a place where 'impressions' occur. It seems that Husserl can be criticised by Sartre for the same reason, as it seems that he considers it as a 'place' where 'cognition' of the objects essence, occurs. Sartre believes that consciousness cannot be a domain in which cognition of object's essence or essential knowledge occurs. If the essential knowledge is considered to be 'immanent' to consciousness and 'transcendental' to the world then it may appear that consciousness is a 'place' where something occurs, and is not simply revealing the world. A brief discussion of Sartre's concept of transcendental ego"[5] can help to explicate this point. Sartre sounds very much unlike Husserl when he says that the self-consciousness of consciousness consists in the consciousness of external world.

The mode of existence of consciousness is to be conscious of itself. And consciousness is consciousness of itself insofar as it is consciousness of a transcendent object. The object of "intentional" act of consciousness transcends this act in that I am conscious of it as not an "immanent" or subjective component of the act itself.[6]

Consciousness cannot be its own object and consciousness cannot be without an external object. Pure consciousness for Sartre is not that which is devoid of external object but is the 'absolute' where "to be" that to exist and 'to appear' that to reveal external object are united. Consciousness exists as a consciousness of external world. Sartre does not believe in reflecting consciousness as to judge it apart from the object of appearance of which it is conscious. Sartre criticises Descartes for considering a reflective consciousness which can reflect consciousness "to think". Sartre holds that by considering a reflecting consciousness to reflect upon the consciousness which thinks, there seems to be a superimposition of a reflecting consciousness on the reflected consciousness. Sartre argues that to hold that consciousness can 'reflect' itself "to think", implies that consciousness which is 'reflecting' does not think. Sartre does not agree with Husserl who believes in an indissoluble unity between a reflecting consciousness and the consciousness reflected upon. Sartre believes only in a non-reflecting consciousness, which finds itself about the external world only.

Consciousness for Sartre cannot exist without being the consciousness of the evanescent world appearing through its present phase and past phase. Sartre's thought has a subtle distinction from Husserl. For Sartre, so long there is consciousness of present there is no chance of being conscious of its own. The "enduring sound" for Husserl is thought to be constituted by "immanent consciousness" by uniting "now phase" and "past phase" as a single object not by depending on its temporal phases. Contrarily, in memory, for Sartre, though the object of thought is equipped with an 'I' but this 'I' is "unreflective" I of 'pre-reflective' consciousness.[7]

> This consciousness must not be posited as an object of my reflection: I must instead direct my attention to the object I am reviving, but *without loosing sight* of the unreflected consciousness.

Thus Sartre will not blank on the "reflection" for the cognition of the enduring sound. Transcendental consciousness is transcendental to itself an "impersonal spontaneity" by which all kinds of cognitions occur.

This "spontaneity" which constantly keeps consciousness engaged in the world, causes "anguish" in consciousness. Consciousness is in anguish because the wish of having a complete world and thereby a permanent self is not satisfied in finite time.

> There is something anguishing in each of us, to experience directly this tireless creation of an existence of which we are not creators. At this level man has the impression of ceaselessly escaping from himself, of overflowing himself... The Me cannot cope with this spontaneity, *for the will is an object which itself is constituted for and by this spontaneity* – Consciousness is terrified of its own spontaneity because it feels its spontaneity as beyond freedom.[8]

This dissatisfaction can be avoided by bringing in the idea of 'ego' but which is 'impossible' for Sartre. Not of course in a traditional sense but if Sartre has to believe in a pure consciousness, he would believe it to be constitutive of 'anguish'. Consciousness cannot be described as a permanent 'anguish'. It is this anguish – which seems to be constitutive of pure consciousness – holds the key to sychological disturbance. If the "I" of the "I think" is the primary structure of consciousness, this anguish is impossible.[9]

Sartre finds this 'anguish' to be the "permanent motive" in "phenomenological reduction". It seems that the "possibility to reach the object by consciousness, which is the source of all "perplexity", motivates Husserl for "phenomenological reduction". But it is a sign of an escapist doctrine of the "phenomenologist" according to Sartre.

> ... For centuries we have not felt in philosophy so realistic a trend. The phenomenologist plunged man back in the world, have given full weight to his anguish ... unfortunately as long as "I" remains a structure of absolute consciousness, phenomenology can still be reproached for providing an escapist doctrine, for drawing a piece of man out of the world and thereby turning our attention away from the real problems. It seems to me that this reproach no longer has any justification if 'Me' is made an existent strictly contemporaneous with the world ...[10]

What is praise-worthy of phenomenologist, for Sartre is their concept of "intentionality" of consciousness that is always of some external object but what is reproachable, is its idea of "immanent cognition" which gives rise to the "phenomenological reduction" according to which the "existence" of the world is to be "bracketed".

Pierre Thevenaz points out that in phenomenology, "to reduce" does not mean to eliminate or to put the world of reality into doubt, but the purpose of 'reduction' is to bring to light the "essential intentional contact" between consciousness and the world which is veiled in naturalistic description. This "reduction" must lead to the 'I' which is transcendental evidence for all knowledge of world phenomenon. This "I" is not identical to the "indubitable I" of Descartes in a doubtful world. This "transcendental subjectivity" is its "apodectic evidence" since it alone is the origin of all meanings. Thevenaz interprets phenomenology of Husserl, primarily as epistemological, next as transcendental and as ontological. Epistemological since at first it is concerned about self evident knowledge for which Husserl believes in apodectic evidence of consciousness which has essential cognition of the world. Next it transcends itself from the existential world. Ontological since he does not find Husserl to take world as "constructed by consciousness".

> The object is not constructed by this consciousness: it gives itself or reveals itself to the view of this consciousness. Here we go boldly any realism or idealism ... the object and the thing is already given essentially tied to consciousness by intentionality.[11]

Thevenaz thinks that phenomenology invites us for transcendental seeing or transcendental experience. By this instead of being lost in the world of objects, a reflection is possible just on the intentional act.

From the above discussion it is clear that Sartre differs from Husserl at least in three respects. First, he does not believe in any state of consciousness or 'I' as a 'reflecting' one. There is only 'pre-reflective' consciousness. It can be judged as transcendental to itself. Such consciousness cannot give any "apodectic evidence" to any knowledge. Second, Sartre finds the idea of 'concrete ego as an escapism of phenomenologist from the anguished spontaneity of consciousness. Third, Sartre opposes "phenomenological reduction" since he finds the "reduction as denial of the "intentional character of consciousness which actually overflows itself to reach out its object. Thus if Thevenaz interprets that Husserl phenomenology guards consciousness from being lost in the intentional world, Sartre's philosophy finds consciousness as lost in the world of intentionality.

In M. K. Bhadra's interpretation of Sartre's difference from phenomenological method of Husserl, he points out how Sartre thinks that Husserl has liberated us from "inward life" and directed us to the reality of world of objects but he was not "true" to the experience of the 'given'[12]. M.K. Bhadra points out two conclusions from Sartre's criticism of Husserl's idea of "transcendental ego". First, that consciousness is ontologically "nothing" as it exists as the consciousness of the world. Second, ontological characteristics of consciousness, depends on the different aspects of conscious experience. Bhadra thus contends that Sartre's phenomenological method has elements both from Husserl and Heidegger.

In Thevenz's writing we find detail examination of the phenomenological method of Heidegger. For Thevenaz though ontology is established in transcendental direction by an effort of the phenomenologist, it is more explicit in Heidegger's philosophy. Phenomenology is concerned with the thing as phenomena and not as opposed to the "thing-in-itself" but the thing-in-itself is 'bracketed'. So the phenomenon which concerns phenomenology is immanent to consciousness. This tendency is interpreted by the disciples of Husserl as a shift from "realism" to "idealism". Heidegger's approach is considered as more ontological in this regard. Apart from accepting phenomenological idea of uncovering the reality through phenomena, Heidegger is considered by Thevenaz to have a deeper inquiry than phenomenology. If Husserl inquires about the foundation of phenomenal world, Heidegger inquires about the "foundation of the foundation".[13] Husserlian recourse of the problem of foundation is too subjective for Heidegger. Heidegger goes beyond consciousness to make it less personal and more ontological that is to 'Dasein' which means "being there". 'There' does not mean a 'place'. Thevenaz accepts Biemel's interpretation of 'Dasein', according to which it is a fundamental structure by means of which man is open to something. Unlike M. K. Bhadra, Thevenaz finds Husserl's discussion to end in "lived experience" since for Husserl, being is revealed to consciousness. Similarly, Heidegger is considered to hold 'Dasein' as a manifestation of a self revealing being. This manifestation occurs through "man's being in the world". Thevenaz points out Heidegger's condemnation of the phenomenological effort to reach the foundation of metaphysics by 'bracketing' empirical evidence.

Thus it seems that for Heidegger, it is "Being" which is self-manifesting to man and illuminates man's own being to him.

> ... man is not the lord of being, he is the shepherd of being"[14]

Thus Heidegger bases human reality not on transcendental consciousness but on transcendental Being.

Husserl-Heidegger-Sartre – A Critiques

From the above discussion of different authors' interpretation, it appears that Sartre differs from Husserl since he dropped "phenomenological reduction". From Sartre's own criticism of phenomenology, it seems that he is closer to Heidegger. But Thevenaz interprets Sartre's dropping of phenomenological reduction as "radicalisation of reduction". For Thevenaz, Heidegger tries to get rid of the subjectivistic attitude of Husserl, consisting in the notion of the transcendental consciousness as an evidence for the knowledge of the external world. Heidegger tried to introduce a concept of 'Being' which is self-illuminating which illuminates the consciousness too. But for Thevenaz, while attacking the "transcendental ego", Sartre adopts the method of reduction only. Husserl reduces world or existence to a "meaning" constituted by consciousness. Sartre reduces consciousness to a 'nothingness', since it has nothing in itself but a drive towards the world. Thevenaz holds that Heidegger rejects "ego consciousness" of Husserl by introducing the idea of "self-revealing Dasein". Sartre seems to save Husserl from Heideggerian attack by rejecting 'ego' and positing consciousness as 'nothingness'.

It seems that Husserlian 'ego' is "transcendental concreteness"; 'transcendental' since it is not related to particular empirical fact, 'concrete' since it is 'essentially' related to the world as a domain of "essential cognition" of the world. Sartre's consciousness can save Husserl from Heideggerian attack and from its being "too subjective", by considering consciousness as "transcendental nothingness". It is a detachment from itself as well as from the fullness of the 'existential' world. Dorothia Frede,[15] while comparing the phenomenological method of Heidegger with that of the Husserl, argues that Heidegger is a "transcendental objectivist as compared to Husserl who is a "transcendental subjectivist". Husserl holds consciousness or ego to be the condition for all determination of the object for experience and thought. Frede thinks that Heidegger accepts Husserl's view that the sense of 'being' of entities consists in our understanding of them. But Heidegger does not accept Husserl's view of 'subject' as transparent ego or as that much impersonal that all ontology can centre around it. Heidegger does not accept that 'bracketing' of the experiential world is possible: he finds 'immanentism' as mistaken. Rather, Heidegger believes that it is the experiential world which transcends consciousness.

Frede gives reasons in favour of Heidegger's opposition to Husserl. First, in ego-centric ontology there can be the influence of personal interest, so Heidegger believes in a general historical situation where there is no place for personal 'I' which underlies all acts of consciousness. Thus he adopts a method of systematic suspicion which is just opposite to 'Cartesian doubt', holds that it is not the external world but the 'I' which is not transparent to ourselves. Heidegger does not think that phenomenon can simply be read off as it is given to consciousness. He looks for the phenomenon that is beyond the surface. The task for Heidegger was to uncover the covered or hidden phenomena. Frede describes Heidegger's phenomenology as 'unhiddenness' which is based on the form of 'disclosedness' in general. Heidegger distinguishes between 'ontic' and 'ontological' level of phenomenological description. 'Ontic' level is that which is open to observation, 'ontological' level is the deep structure that explains 'ontic'.

Heidegger considers the analysis of human existence to be the primary stage of his method since he finds human understanding to be the sole medium to know the nature of being which he considers to be the authentic existence of man. For Heidegger there cannot be any self-awareness without the awareness of the world. For such awareness he introduced the term 'Dasein'. 'Dasein' means that our being open to the world. Thus for Heidegger the key to understand the being, is the openness of the being in the world which gives rise to a general fundamental ontology. It becomes clear why Heidegger finds the 'bracketing' of the world to be impossible. World for Heidegger is precisely the context in which we find being and ourselves.

Harrison Hall[16] shows how Heidegger tries to estrange himself from Husserl but ultimately joins phenomenological tradition. Hall finds Heidegger to accept Husserl's view of philosophy as "rigorous science" to get things as they really are. But he refuses to consider the sense of the object as a "perceptual cognition" but as being 'manipulated'.

> The kind of dealing which is closure to us is – not a bare perceptual consciousness but rather that kind of concern that manipulates things and put them to use. (BT 95)[17]

> Dasein finds "itself" proximally in what it does, uses, expects, avoids – in those things environmentally "ready to hand" with which it is proximally *concerned*. (BT 155)[18]

Heidegger describes the object as "ready to hand" as they are in the ordinary way in our practical activity, the intentionality of practical activity is directed towards the world of object not in terms of perception of object around but in terms of practical interest and concern. Hall points out that the concept of the concern of the worlds is derived from the practical world. The world given in perception cannot be the basis to construct a practical world out of it.*

Heidegger describes the Husserlian world as "present to hand" constructed on a basis of meaning of it, grasped by

---

* Sartre seems to unite the world of perception and practical world since for him the world of exigencies is given in perception. Moreover, for Sartre perception is intentional purposive.

consciousness. Hall interprets Heideggerian world as "ready to hand" and not to be derived from the Husserlian world. It gives the impression that the meaning is not considered with similar implication by both of them. Hall finds Heideggerian world as a result of 'subtraction' of interest and involvement from practical world. He also points out that if practical activity breaks down by subtracting personal interest it cannot lead to a commitment towards Husserlian world. Hall interprets that Heidegger's view of practical world which is constructed by the relation of practical activity, indicates a prior grasping of more general human activity in a general worldly structure. The specific activities are particular cases of general world-hood. Thus from Heideggerian perspective, human way of being is conceived in the broadest sense.

From the above discussion of Frede and Hall, we get to understand that if Husserl is "transcendental subjectivist" Heidegger is "practical objectivist". We can call him to be an objectivist, since he seems to believe in a general world-hood as a way of being. Hall pointed out that the general world-hood should not imply any impersonal understanding of man. Heidegger condemns inauthentic understanding of man. Inauthentic understanding, for Heidegger, is 'absorption' of man in the public world by the norms that constitute it. Here Hall finds Heidegger to join Husserl and arrive at the ontology of "present – to hand".[19]

To conclude from the above discussion, we find that Husserl starts viewing the human reality from the essential knowledge of consciousness, 'brackets' the existential world and believes in the world as a 'meaning' grasped by consciousness. But Heidegger, on the other hand, starts viewing human reality as a relation with the world that is outside consciousness. He considers the world as a general context for all men and being. He believes in the authentic understanding of the world which cannot be in general or public but subjective. Heidegger seems to differentiate between the 'being-in-the-world' and understanding of the 'being-in-the-world'. We could say that at first he believes in a general ontology where being shows man in itself but finally he took refuge into a subjective epistemology for the understanding of their being.

Sartre seems to reconcile between subjectivity and objectivity of human life from the very beginning by considering consciousness as 'nothing' in itself. It exists as a consciousness of the external world. Even self consciousness for Sartre consists in the consciousness of the world. Thus consciousness indicates 'nothingness'. The world or the object of consciousness which is not nothing but 'being' is separated from consciousness forever in Sartre's philosophical purpose as to establish the non-duality of subject and object, it is better to describe his purpose as to reconcile between two. Actually they are separated but ontologically or epistemologically they are united that is in order to explicate reality or to know the reality there is no way but to reconcile between two which are separated for ever.

Thevenaz holds that Sartre's "phenomenological ontology" is not a movement towards 'being', 'being' is 'nihilated' from consciousness. Phenomenological method is lost in such 'reduction'.

> The "phenomenological ontology" of Being and Nothingness is not a method of progressive movement towards being. The reduction in the form of nihilation is so radical that phenomenology is swept away at the same time.[20]

Our purpose in this chapter is to develop Sartre's method, which interprets human consciousness as a ceaseless effort to grasp trans-phenomenal being. Trans-phenomenal since it is not reduced to its finite series of appearance or phenomena grasped by consciousness. We accept Thevenaz's interpretation partly as we do not say that Sartre's phenomenological ontology of consciousness accepts grasp ability of the trans-phenomenal being. But it seems that Sartre's method definitely shows consciousness as an effort which tries to grasp 'being', the effort is not however 'progressive'. We can seek the help of Murdoch's analysis in this regard.[21] Murdoch sees Sartre to picture consciousness by means of two contrasts between the flickering, unstable, semitransparent moment to moment being of the consciousness, the shifting way in which it conceives object and itself and the solid opaque inert in-themselves of things which simply are what they are. Consciousness is not "empty self awareness" since it is not reflecting but unreflectively engaged in grasping the world. Murdoch holds that the "Supreme value" towards which consciousness, by its very nature, is transcending, is the "absolute being" of the self for its quality of 'identity' and 'permanence', but fails.[22]

Thus unlike Thevenaz we like to point out that Husserl's consciousness is detached from the object, as a "place of the essential cognition of the object, whereas Sartre's consciousness, is detached from the object, as a 'nothingness' but exists as a consciousness of object only. If ontologically consciousness is a nothingness as a detachment from the world, it is a 'nothingness', also by being an attachment to the world and not to itself. In this way Sartre's philosophy expresses a paradox in the being of the consciousness. It seems that for Sartre consciousness is a 'nothingness' since it is always a drive towards out-side world but simply a drive without ever being able to grasp the being. It cannot grasp being, if it can grasp, it will no more remain a consciousness but will turn into an object. So it seems that the being for which it aims must not be a being similar to the being of the object. Thus about the existence of consciousness, Sartre's view is more or less similar to Heidegger.

> To say consciousness is consciousness of something is to say it must produce itself as a revealed revelation of being which is not it and which gives itself as already existing when consciousness reveals it" [23]

The point which makes Sartre's method different from the method of Heidegger is that for Sartre 'being' can be the source of the revelation of consciousness in so far as it is 'nihilated' by consciousness. This nihilation is not considered by Heidegger. Another point of Sartre's philosophical method expresses his inclination to accept Husserlian method when Sartre explicates the possibility of taking different perspectives by consciousness of external world which makes the world evanescent.

> "It would require an infinite process to inventory the total content of a thing."[24]

Like Heidegger, Sartre does not believe that consciousness is revealed by the being rather being is revealed by the consciousness. Being cannot be self-revealing and it is revealed as being 'nihilated' because it is consciousness which surpasses being infinitely. Thus it seems that the revelation of the world becomes an infinite process due to consciousness.

> Yet the existent in fact cannot be reduced to a *finite* series of manifestations since each one of them is a relation to subject constantly changing. Although an object may disclose itself only through a single *Abschattung*, the sole fact of there being a subject implies possibility of multiplying the point of view on the *Abschattung*.[25]

In this connection it seems that Sartre is neither too subjectivist, like Husserl, nor he asserts revelation, like Heidegger to be an objective fact. For Sartre 'being' is not self-revealing, it is self existing. Consciousness too cannot exist without being a revelation of 'being'. But it does not allow at the same time 'being' to be revealed in a finite time. Thus we find reconciliation between subjective interpretation and objective interpretation of consciousness, by Sartre.

Our purpose in this chapter is to point out how Sartre is describing consciousness as a drive to grasp being and at the same time as a failure in grasping it. In *Emotion*, we find Sartre discussing the process of aspiration of consciousness. We must first explain a confusion, which arises in this connection. In Emotion on Sartre, while distinguishing "philosophical method', from "psychology" seems to accept the method of "phenomenological reduction" what he condemns in The *Transcendence of The ego*, since for him it is an escape from the anguished spontaneity of consciousness.

> ... the idea of man can no longer be an empirical concept, the product of historical generalisation, son the contrary, we have to use the a priori essence of human being ... psychic facts we meet are never the first ones. They are in their essential structure. Therefore, they assume man and the world and can only take on their true meaning... If we wish to find a psychology, we shall have to go beyond man's situation in the world, to the very source of man, the world and the psychic: the transcendental and the consecutive consciousness which we attain by "phenomenological reduction" or putting the world in "parenthesis".[26]

Contrarily, he holds in The *Transcendence of The ego* that "phenomenological reduction" is a learned operation[27] based on the reflective operation of consciousness as to transcend 'I' in order to have a self. But Sartre does not believe in reflective observation of consciousness what we have already discussed. Thus he does not accept either the empirical observation of psychic facts which is the method of psychology in discovering human nature or the reflective observation of the activity of consciousness. It seems that the stand he takes in *Emotion* is to refute the method of psychology, for his preference even for "phenomenological reduction" instead of empirical observation. According to M.K. Bhadra, Sartre's own method is different from both Husserl and Heidegger since it is a "dynamic phenomenology"[28] finds consciousness always to surpass the present. This surpassing is not to 'bracket' the present world to reach another present world.

> ...action as spontaneous unreflective consciousness and that in order to act it is not necessary to be

> conscious of self as acting - quite the contrary, in short, unreflective behaviour is not unconscious behaviour; it is conscious of itself non-thetically, and its way of being thetically conscious of itself is to transcend itself and to seize upon the world as a quality of things.[29]

According to the 'exigencies' and 'desire' of man, human actions directed to the world is actually aimed at world in a narrow sense for Sartre. He uses a German word 'unwelt'[30] which seems to indicate a world of need. Another important thing which is there in Sartre's discussion of human action and desire is 'perception'. Sartre thinks that "the world as a quality of things" is given to man in his 'perception' and he denies the possibility of reflection in finding it to be 'difficult'.

> This world is difficult this notion of difficulty is not reflective notion which would imply a relationship to me. It is there on the world; it is a quality of the world which is given in the perception; - it is noematical correlative of our activity undertaken or only conceived.[31]

World is difficult for Sartre since it is "out there" and not within us. We can understand world through the needful object such as books, shoes etc. At the same time, we understand object as having essence which we lack. It is a 'noematic correlative' of our action since our action is an effort to have "essence". Now the question arises whether the object in its completeness which is not grasped but desired to be grasped, is imagined or induced?

Being is Induced or Imagined

The world from which our desire stems out is an empirical one. We like to interpret Sartre's method of philosophising from the perspective of empirical knowledge. But Sartre does not intend to interpret our desire on the basis of empirical evidence.

The original project which is expressed in each of our empirically observable tendencies is then the project of being, or, - each empirical tendency exists within the original project of being, in a relation of expression and a symbolic satisfaction just as consciousness drives with Freud, exist in relation to the original libido, Fundamentally, man is the desire to be and the existence of the desire is not to be established by an empirical induction. It is the result of an a priori description.[32]

We could raise a question against Sartre that how can he draws a similarity of his concept of fundamental project with Freud's concept of Libido? He cannot say that ultimate project is totally hidden from us, but he could say we do not have clear consciousness of the "fundamental project". Freud's concept of 'libido' implies a hidden desire not expressed rather suppressed. Sartre as a phenomenologist cannot accept anything as hidden reality. M.K. Bhadra in his thesis points out that.

> Sartre could say we do not have a clear consciousness of it. So it is to be grasped from a study of the individual projects which again, can be understood better in relation to the fundamental project.[33]

We can say that individual project or the projects that are empirically observable can be studied as particular desire for particular object given in perception. Empirically it cannot be studied as manifestations of 'fundamental' desire. Here we could discuss how Sartre describes 'perception' by comparing it with 'conception'.

> The immediate consciousness which I have of perception does not permit me either to judge or to will — all that, there is of intention in my actual consciousness and is directed towards outside, toward the world.[34]

So perception is a 'spontaneous' relationship of consciousness to the world and it is 'pre-reflective'.

> In perception I observe object - object enters into my consciousness in its completeness. I nevertheless see it only from one side at a time... I must therefore apprehend them successively, the characteristic of a perception is that the object appears only in a series of profiles... The perception of an object is thus a phenomenon of an infinity of aspects. When on the other hand, I think of a cube by means of a concrete concept... I seize it in its entirety at one glance.[35]

Sartre considers 'conception' as a means to form "image" which is a subjective image, not actual.

> No matter how long I look at an image, I shall never find anything in it but what I put there.[36]

Sartre points out that the object of 'image' is not an "actual object" but since it is a "conceptual object" it can be grasped at "one glance". For the actual object Sartre holds that consciousness needs to have "infinite time".

> In the world of perception every thing has an infinite number of relationship to other thing which constitutes the very essence of thing.[37]

Another dimension which we know about the object of an "image" is that the object posited in image is absent in actuality.

> ... object of the image *as long as it is imagined* differs in nature from the type of existence of the object grasped as real. If I now form an Image of Peter - as he is now at this moment in Berlin or in London... But while he appears to me as an image, this Peter who is in London *appears to me absent*. This absence in actuality, this essential nothingness of imagined object, is enough to distinguish from the object of perception.[38]

In case of perception, a part of a thing can be "hidden" to our intuition. If only the legs of chair are visible, through the window, they are perceived on the context of a chair, legs are perceived only as a part of the whole. Sartre holds that in case of 'image' the absence is 'grasped' in case of 'perception'; on the contrary object is not absent but given as "hidden" from which consciousness is detached for the moment, at the same time directed towards the 'hidden' that is towards the 'whole' object.

> ... there is a great difference in *being grasped as nothing and being given as absent*. In perception of whatever sort many empty intentions are directed from the element now given, towards other aspects and other elements of the object which no longer reveals themselves to our institution... in this sense to perceive it on the foundation of total reality as *a whole*.[39]

'Image' and 'perception' are radically different for Sartre; 'image' is positing an 'absent' so grasps it at one glance, whereas 'perception' is observation of the "real", successively, which is given as a whole but 'hidden' to consciousness.

> The hypothesis of the imaginative consciousness is radically different from the hypothesis of consciousness of real.[40]

But for Sartre, consciousness of 'real' serves the foundation for the consciousness of "imagination". The world of perception is a 'situation' given to consciousness.

> ... every concrete and real situation of consciousness in the world is pregnant with imagination in as much as it always present itself as withdrawing from the rear. It does not follow that all perception of the real must reverse itself in imagination, but as consciousness is always "in situation" because it is always free, it always and each moment has the concrete possibility of producing the unreal.[41]

We can say that it is possible that the process of grasping

Being or the "project of being" is the original project expressed in all particular project, originates from the world of 'perception' that is from the empirical world of 'real'. In this world of 'perception' the perception in 'profiles' or in parts may lead to the unknown parts. Sartre believes that this process is possible as the parts are always realised in the context of the whole. 'Perception' is a 'successive' process of grasping the real world. In this connection, we find Sartre believing in 'induction' to grasp the 'future', the unperceived real, through 'anticipation'.

> When I play tennis, I see my opponent hit the ball with his racket and I run to the net. Here, there is anticipation since I foresee the course of the ball. But this anticipation does not posit for itself the passage of the ball to this or that point. In reality the future is here only as the *real* development of a form induced by the gesture of my opponent communicates its reality to the whole form.[42]

It seems that the future which is induced is not to anticipate the specific line or length of the ball but the totality of the gesture of the opponent in which he communicates. It seems that we go from a particular 'hit' at the ball to the whole gesture. The question arises that if the world or 'perception' apprehends future by inducing it and if it is the possible ground of "imagination" can induction explain the process of consciousness directed towards "not yet" or towards 'being' which consciousness tries to acquire? The question arises that if consciousness can anticipate 'hidden' whole by inducing it from the perceived part, can consciousness imagine absent world by ınducing it from the perceived real part of the world? Here we should note that induction cannot give us any knowledge of the future which is not contained in the 'present'. We can now see whether Sartre is actually philosophising through the method of inductive inference or not. He believes that we are not inducing a new future from the present in case of anticipation. Future represents a 'form' in which present is perceived.

There is no doubt that his method cannot be deductive. The present is in no way derivable from the future or the 'form'. He considers the possibility of inducing it. We have raised the question can Sartre's concept of imagination or "ultimate project" be interpreted through the method of inductive inference? We will try to see whether the same induction can interpret Sartre's philosophising of the positing of not yet which actually represents the ontological structure of consciousness and characterises the ultimate project of man.

> ... the person is crushed in the world, run through by the real, he is closest to the thing. However, as soon as he apprehends in one way or another – the whole as a *situation* he retreats from towards that in relation to which he is a *lack* ...[43]

Although Sartre says that the consciousness of the 'image' is radically different from the consciousness of the 'real' but he has based the former on the latter. It seems for Sartre there is a single process of consciousness which starts from the world of perception, being directed towar.ds its object of desire or need, goes with the tension and anxiety of this directedness which is without pause or rest and tries to change the world and posits and end which is "not yet" or absent.

Sartre accepts induction have seen that he rejects that empirical observation of human action can interpret human reality as a 'lack'. Therefore, he would not accept that induction is a method undergone by consciousness to posit an absent in imagination. He thinks that only through a priori description it is possible to establish human reality as a 'lack'. A priori description of the particular project can judge the end posited by particular project. And we can say that it is not through, observing consciousness through 'perception' he induce the characteristics of 'imagination'. It seems that by observing consciousness, through its 'imagination' Sartre describes it as 'lack'. "Imagination" cannot be observed empirically not even reflectively. Sartre considers his method to be a priori description. In the philosophy of history we find that "a priorism" leads to 'certainty' and in this context it seems that Sartre is traditional enough to consider knowledge of the 'imagination' to be 'certain'. But we should not be oblivious of the fact that Sartre does not believe in certainty of knowledge 'in actuality'. So the certainty which is considered in the case of imagination is not actual certainty, he considers certainty of knowledge posited by imagination as 'absent'.

> It is one thing to describe image and quite another to draw a conclusion regarding its nature in going from one to another, we pass from certainty to probability.[44]

In perception for Sartre, knowledge is probable we actually undergo an apprenticeship without knowing the thing with certainty. Thus it seems that if induction is a method that starts from certainty and ends in probability, Sartre's philosophising starts from probability of knowledge in perception, and ends in 'certainty' of imagination. Moreover, the emotion that works in Sartre's description of consciousness, is not for grasping the evanescent world but for making itself a 'lack' by bringing 'nothingness' into the world and by positing an object which is "not yet", to change the world which appears too difficult by surpassing infinitely every effort to grasp it, emotion is not to grasp the whole but to change the existing whole.

> ... emotion is transformation of the world when the path traced out become too difficult or when we see no path, we can no longer live in so difficult a world. So we try to change the world.[45]

Another difficulty we will face in interpreting Sartre's philosophy through inductive inference is that we can not reconcile between the subjective and the objective interpretation of Husserl and Heidegger respectively which seems to be intended by Sartre. This effort of reconciliation by Sartre will be ignored in interpreting Sartre's philosophy through inductive method.

In induction on the basis of particular evidences universal, conclusion is drawn in probability. In Sartre's ontology, every profile is perceived in the context of the whole, there is no question of deriving the whole from the particulars, when the universal is derived from the particulars in induction, a leap is taken from the particular to conclude in universal. No such leap is taken in Sartre's philosophising in conceiving the whole as a context to the particular perception. The only similarity what matters is that in inductive inference particular facts are considered as contingent fact, so proving universals as probable truth. In Sartre's philosophy also particular facts are accidental and they are necessarily manifesting the whole but due to the infinite appearance of particular facts, the knowledge of the whole is always probable knowledge. But it is clear that Sartre's philosophy does not conceive any actual duality between subjective particular appearance and objective totality. But when an absent 'certainty' is 'imagined' we don't derive it from the probable knowledge of perception but we take a leap. In case of perception, subjective particular perception is expressing the objective totality in profiles but in case of imagination, subjectivity is separating itself from the non-duality of subjective and objective knowledge. The whole context which is expressed by the particular perception is superseded by the imagined whole. But actually it seems that imagination is an expression of human emotion raised from the unfulfillment of the perceptual world. The subjective imagination which posit 'absent' with 'certainty', definitely comes out of the infinity of the perceptual world. This infinity comes from human emotion. By explicating man's desire to get the certainty of the imagined world in his perceptual world, Sartre is explaining the unity between the whole and the parts of human consciousness which is nothing but an aspiration for a complete being.

We have argued first, that Sartre has reconciled between subjectivity and objectivity in describing consciousness as nothing in itself. Second, reconciliation between perception and imagination is also worked out since Sartre actually founded his imagination on 'perception'. Though perception and conception are radically separated but they belong to the same process of consciousness. Third, since imagination which actually bring 'nothingness' into the world by positing an 'absent' reality, is based on the perception, and since in perception we find 'future' to be included as the 'hidden' 'form' of the present perception, an apparent similarity of Sartre's method with induction is worked out. Fourth, the difficulties are pointed out in interpreting Sartre's method of philosophy as inductive inference since induction is a method that starts from the certainty of perception and concludes in probability, on the other hand, Sartre's concept of consciousness brings 'nothingness' into the world by positing an 'absent' 'certainty' on the basis of the probability' of knowledge. It seems that Sartre's a priori method does not indicate any effort to establish a metaphysical truth that is beyond empirical world. His method describes consciousness as that which transcends the world of 'perception' in imagination but takes its elements from the perception.

Sartre's consciousness is never without the empirical 'situation' but is always an effort to overcome it. So the world of perception is discussed with much importance in Sartre's philosophy. In the next chapter we propose to discuss Sartre's method by considering the human reality as "particular projects" or action. We have already noticed that human reality brings 'nothingness' actually being motivated by the world of perception which man surpasses forever. The chapter will also concentrate on the human "situation" that starts from the "particular project". Particular projects are empirically observable projects which stem out of the empirical world which is given in perception, directed to acquire something which is there in the empirical world. Perception by virtue of being an infinite process is to be directed to the world forever. It reduces man into particular projects. The next chapter will try to focus on this characteristic of "human situation" to get more aspects of Sartre's method of philosophising.

References

1. Husserl Edmnnd, *Train of Throughout in the Lectures* from April 26 to May.
2. 1950 in Gotingen Tr. By W. Atston, Ed. By G. Nakhnikian, 1969, pp 2-5.
3. *Ibid.*, pp. 8-10,
4. PI., p. 2,
5. TE., pp. 40-49,
6. TE., pp. 42-47,
7. TE., p. 45,
8. *Ibid.*, p. 1000,
9. TE., p. 106,
10. *Ibid.*, p. 106,
11. P. Thevenaz P. What is Phenomenology. Ed with intro by J. Edie Quadreangle book Inc. Chicago 1962 p 50.
12. Bhadra, M.K., *A Critical Study of Sartre's Ontology of Consciousness,* Univ. Burdwan, 1978 p. 9.
13. Thevenaz P., *What is Phenomenology,* p. 52.
14. Ibid. p. 59.
15. Frede D. Cambridge Companion to Heidegger, Ed by C. B. Guignon, Camnridge Univ. Press 1993, pp. 52-56.
16. Hall, H. 'Intentionality and World': (Division I of Being and Time, Cambridge Companion to Heidegger 1993, pp 120-128.
17. *Ibid.*, p. 125,
18. *Ibid.*, p. 126,
19. *Ibid.*, pp 125-139,
20. Thevenaz, P., *What is Phenomenology*, p. 71.
21. Murdoch, I., *Sartre Romantic Rationalist*, Collins, The fountana Library, Bowes and Bowes Ltd. 1952.
22. *Ibid.*, pp. 62-65.
23. BN., p. 24.
24. BN., p. 11.
25. *Ibid.*. p. 5.

26. Emotion, pp. 10-11.
27. TE., pp. 98-106.
28. Bhadra M.K., *A Critical Survey, of Phenomenology and Existentialism*, I.C.P.R, Allied Publishers New, Delhi 1990. p. 345.
29. Emotion, pp. 56-57.
30. *Ibid.,* p. 57.
32. BN., p. 722.
31. *Ibid.,* p. 58.
33. A Critical Study ... M. K. Bhadra, p. 39.
34. BN., p. 12.
35. PT., p. 5.
36. p. 7. PI.
37. *Ibid.*, p. 7.
38. *PI.,* p. 209.
39. *Ibid.,* p. 209.
40. *Ibid.*, pp. 208-209.
41. PI., p. 216.
42. *Ibid.,* p. 211.
43. PI., p. 217.
44. PI., p. 2.
45. Emotion, p. 58.

3

Aspiration and Project –A Human Situation

Man's failure to grasp the whole being seems to be the basis of Sartre's explication of the ontology of consciousness in terms of its transcendence of the being in one hand. On the other hand, it is explicated by the being which is revealed through the unending series of appearances. On the basis of the evidence of the perceived and known fact of appearance of the object, this explication can be alternatively conceived as being based upon an induction, as the form of object is possibly induced by consciousness. Thus a similarity between Sartre's method and inductive method was highlighted in the last chapter. However, at a deeper analysis, it has been tried to show that similarity cannot be sustained. The object posited by consciousness in 'imagination' is an 'absent' object in actuality which is actually based on the human emotion to change the world as it finds the world too difficult which is given in 'perception'. We have discussed in our first chapter that the end posited by consciousness is to acquire a primacy over the being of consciousness which is ceaselessly directed towards the world. By combining two aspirations, one is to change the world and another is to have primacy over the being which is directed to the world, we can hold that the changed world which is graspable at a time, gives man the primacy over his being. The things which are clear in Sartre's concept of human aspiration are three things; first that man aspires to overcome his 'objectification' in the world by him as well as by other; second, man aspires to have a control over his own 'freedom' which is reduced to action and over other who reduces him to object, so to have a being of a 'unique person' and third, the end posited is "absent in actuality". But the thing which is not clear in Sartre's concept of human aspiration is that how Sartre conceives such end to be man's aspiration and how he can considers it to be the sole thing expressed in every human action. The project which becomes explicit through human action is the "particular project", the "fundamental project" conceived by Sartre, is not explicit. The question arises how can he find such end to be the end of human action?

Dialectic between Particular and Global Project

For Sartre human reality is nothing but an 'action'. And human action is not mechanical, it has to be defined by an intention.

> A first glance at human reality informs us that its being is reduced to doing. Thus human reality does not exist in order to act later – the existence of act implies autonomy – act is not pure motion but must be defined by an intention–intention is a choice of end – reveals the world as this or that – is a state of world to be obtained and not yet existing.[1]

Thus man's being indicates an intention, the fulfillment of which is not in itself but there in the external world.

> Consciousness is pure and simple negation of the given and it exists as the disengagement from a certain existing and as an engagement towards a certain not yet existing end.[2]

Such human behaviour which is both engagement and disengagement at a time, is 'project' for Sartre.

> The most rudimentary behaviour – determined both in relation to present factors which condition it and

> in relation to a certain object, still to come, which it is trying to being into being. This is what we call project – in relation to the given praxis is negativity – in relation to the object aimed at praxis is positivity.[3]

It seems that man as a "project" is a withdrawal from itself and an affirmation towards the world. If we have to define man affirmatively in terms of what man is, we have to concentrate on man as a being projected towards the world. This affirmative state for Sartre is "global project".

> Our particular projects are united in global project which we are. But precisely because we are wholly choice and act these particular projects are not determined by the global project. They must themselves be choices; and a certain margin of contingency or unpredictability and of the absurd is allowed to each of them – although each project as it projected is the specification of the global project on the occasion of particular elements in the situation and so is always understood in relation to the totality on my being in the world.[4]

So the particular projects are independent but they cannot be understood or judged independently.

> A coward is defined by the deed he has done – there is every possibility for the coward to give up cowardice... what count is the total commitment and it is not by particular case or particular action that you are committed altogether.[5]

In Sartre's philosophy human reality as "particular projects" cannot determine the being of man, since there may be no continuation in future of that what it has revealed for man. For Sartre man can be revealed by the "total commitment" only. Sartre talks about a "Fundamental principle" to preside over every "particular project".

> The fundamental value which presides over this

> exactly the in - itself - for- itself that is the project is ideal of a consciousness which would be the foundation of its being - in - itself by the pure consciousness which it would have of itself, it is this ideal which can be called God.[6] It is only by making itself for itself that being can aspire to be the cause of itself. Consciousness as the nihilation of being appears therefore at one stage in a progression towards immanence of causality, i.e. towards being a self cause. The progression 'however' stops there as a result of insufficiency of the being in itself. The temporalisation of consciousness which is not an ascending progression towards the dignity of the causa-sui; it is a surface run off whose origin is on tile contrary, the impossibility of being a self cause.[7]

The phrase making itself for itself seems to indicate man's effort to concentrate within itself. But in his effort man goes out-side himself. Man lacks the self for which he aspires. This self is "self-cause" for Sartre. It seems that man wants to be the cause of self. Why man aspires to be the cause of self? This can be answered with the discussion of Sartre's concept of freedom. Sartre holds that man's "freedom" is reduced to action. Freedom implies human action to be 'unconditioned'. In every action man is expressing his freedom. But man has no freedom not to act. He can choose this instead of that but cannot abstain from choosing.

> ...freedom is neither a given nor a property, it can be only by choosing itself. The freedom of for-itself is always *engaged*; ... freedom is simply the fact that choice is always unconditioned. This is because freedom is a choice of its being not the foundation of his being; human reality can choose itself as it intends but is not able not to choose itself.[8]

The phrase possession of his "foundation of itself' indicates a being in man which can have a own being. In this sense, it seems that man tries to possess freedom. For Sartre freedom is not a 'property' of man, it is his being. We can say that "freedom" indicates man's power of doing things independently but no power of not doing things independently. Thus freedom becomes the being of man who is always in action. It is not only distancing itself from the present but acts towards a possibility.

> Thus freedom is discovered only in action and is intimately fused with it ... it is not an innate virtue that gives it license to break away from the most compelling situation ... It is rather the power to commit ourselves to the task at hand and to construct a future.[9]

Man cannot avoid his freedom. He has to undergo his 'unconditioned' choice. His choice is "unconditioned"; he remains responsible for all his actions. We have already discussed that for Sartre, man's action reveals the world as this or that and man remains responsible for everything that happens in the world. Thus freedom as described by Sartre is a burden on man.

> "...essential consequence of man's being condemned to be free carries the weight of the whole world on his shoulders; I am responsible for everything, in fact, except for my very responsibility, for I am not the foundation of my being – as if I were compelled to be responsible. I am *abandoned* in the world ...whatever I do to tear myself away from the responsibility – I am responsible for my very desire of fleeing responsibility".[10]

Thus by having no primacy over his being man finds himself with the burden of "freedom" and "responsibility". From the very beginning of his existence, he finds himself bound to do something with his own choice and to be responsible for it. Man has freedom and responsibility but he has not chosen his being as to be free and responsible thus he finds ... "no pillar no support in what I was"[11].

"What it was" indicates a being of man which is prior to his freedom. In his freedom or in his effort to go out of his being which is "reduced to freedom", man goes out of himself. Man's action implies his going out of himself.

> In order not to be a given for-itself must constitute itself as an withdrawal in relation to itself ...[12]

The only reality which appears as human reality is his action. If we look at Sartre's method, with the view point similar to that of deduction or induction, we cannot interpret the 'fundamental' end or the 'presiding' value of all "particular project" as to change the world in order to have a primacy over man's being. It is clear that Sartre's method cannot be deductive since he believes in the freedom of the "particular project" which cannot be determined by the "fundamental project" or "global project". Moreover, for Sartre every particular project is the expression of "fundamental project", but this fundamental project is not certain. And particular project cannot be deduced from the "fundamental project". To see whether Sartre's method is inductive or not, we can concentrate on the empirically observable "particular project" and the "global project" which is getting designed by the "particular project". For Sartre, as we have already discussed that "particular projects are so accidental or changeable that no human nature can be derived from them. Sartre does not believe in any universal nature but he seems to believe in a universal human purpose.

> "... although it is impossible to find in each a universal human essence that can be called human nature there is nevertheless a human universality of condition. The *limitations a priori* define man's fundamental situation in the universe. His main historical situation is variable. But what never vary are the necessities of being in the world of having to labour and to die there. Every human purpose presents itself as an attempt either to surpass these limitations, or to widen them or else to deny or to

> accommodate oneself to them consequently, every purpose however individual it may be, is of universal value – in every purpose there is universality...[13]

By accepting the variability of the "particular projects", Sartre seems to believe in a static "universal purpose". But as "universal purpose" or "universal human condition" is expressed through the "particular project", there is nothing more in that which is expressed in "universal human condition" or purpose than "particular project" of man. Sartre does not find anything in "universal human purpose" except the infiniteness of human 'labour' throughout his existence. But the question arises why this infiniteness of action is considered to be the "human purpose"? It seems that Sartre considers it a "purpose" as he does not believe in any human action which is not intentional action. Sartre is not actually expressing any universal purpose but the purpose of every particular project that is to go on performing action infinitely throughout the existence of man. For every action there must be an end. But Sartre is not conceiving any static being as human end. Rather he considers human end to surpass his being which is reduced to doing. While surpassing he can only act. The end which provokes man to surpass his being which is reduced to action, keeps man engaged simply in action. Man acts to surpass action and there is actually no difference between man's being which is reduced to doing and man's purpose which keeps him in action. The only difference between the two is that man as a "particular project" is reduced to doing but man as a "purpose" is a primacy over his being which is a "self cause" of his being or action. In Empirical observation we can find man with "particular project" with particular purpose. Empirically we do not observe but can derive from this "particular project a "universal purpose". Moreover, for Sartre one does not have to go from particular project to universal project to understand his universal purpose. Sartre believes that all particular projects being, intentional, express the same intention to be the cause of itself. We have noticed that Sartre does not think that we can understand "particular project" independent of the "global project". But they are not determined by the "global project".

From all this we can draw a philosophical insight, used in Sartre's method which is neither based on the observation of "particular project" which are simply with "particular purpose" nor on the "global project" if it means a 'generality' of human action, from which all particular actions can be derived. Man's global project or universal purpose cannot be equal to man's dreams etc.

> "... man is no other than a series of undertakings – dreams, expectation and hopes define man as deceptive dreams, abortive hopes, expectations unfulfilled; that is to say they define him negatively not positively.[14]

Dreams, hopes etc. together do not indicate universal human purpose. Dreams etc. define man negatively whereas universal purpose or global project defines man as what he is.

It is interesting to note Steven Barbone article[15] in this respect. His point is that Sartre is assuming a "fundamental project", i.e., to be God which can explain all actions and behaviours as only one project for each individual which unifies and unites all his actions towards a single goal. Unification does not come after 'diversity', for Sartre. Barbone considers "fundamental project to be logically prior. But Barbone's view cannot be accepted. If the "fundamental project" is logically prior to particular project, the particular project can be derived from fundamental project, this derivability is not acceptable to Sartre. Barbone makes another point that the notion of "fundamental project" raises the problem of unconscious in Sartre's philosophy. But we should not be oblivious of the fact that man knows the fundamental project a priori. To interpret human reality in terms of a "fundamental project" a method is required which is neither inductive nor deductive nor phenomenological. It is not even Freudian but a much broader view which can grasp human reality as reconciliation between particular action and universal action.

> ... a single act can be evaluated at more and more complex level and that consequently it is expressed by a series of very diverse significance. One should not conclude that this signification remain independent, separated, so to speak, by impassable distances the signification of super structure are produced in terms of substructure.[16]

Sartre also says that self surpassing acts of man cannot be interpreted as "instances" of surpassing, He says.

> "This surpassing is not instantaneous movement, it is long works. For this reasons life develops in spirals; it passes again and again by the same points but at different levels of integration and complexity."[17]

Some logicians interpret deductive inference as instantaneous. But particulars in inductive inference are not instances but expressions. There are ample reasons to interpret Sartre's philosophical method as inductive inference since it seems that by observing particular project empirically, by seeing their infiniteness Sartre has induced an end common to all man or a "universal human purpose" that is to act till death. It seems as if the "global project" is conceived as the universality of particular project. It is due to the necessary relation between particular and universal in human project. In induction there is no necessary relation between particular facts and universal conclusion, there is a leap from particular to universal, so universal indicates probability in relation to particular. In Sartre's philosophy a particular projects is necessarily an expression of "universal project"; it is not of course similar to the concept of necessity upheld in deductive inference. Sartre makes it clear that "particular projects" are not derivable from 'universal' or "global project", "particular projects', are unpredictable for Sartre. But when this "universal human purpose" or 'condition' or the "fundamental project" or "global project" is interpreted as a project to be God of itself which almost rules out the possibility to interpret Sartre's philosophy as inductive inference. Empirically man's particular projects cannot be judged as a project of being a God. This project has to be intuited. Moreover, Sartre ultimately makes a point that human aspiration is not a linear movement, it moves like a 'spiral'. Induction moves from particular to universal whereas universal in Sartre philosophy seems to be at the centre of the particular actions from which actions move up in a circular manner, so cannot be defined by induction. We shall discuss about this spiral later in this chapter. To understand the fundamental and universal human purpose which is the lone human purpose for every human action, it requires a profound experience regarding human reality.

This experience should not be considered as transcendental or metaphysical. Rather it is based on the experience of man who finds the empirical world difficult to which he is always directed and tries to acquire it as a quality of things. Its infinite possibility cannot allow him to acquire the world at a time, so he tries to be the "foundation" of itself. In this experience 'other' plays a very crucial role. Man is actually thrown into a social-historical world" which will be discussed in a different chapter. For the time being we should note that Sartre's method seems to be an experiential method. Thus the criticism against Sartre that his philosophy gives rise to the problem of "unconscious" is not justified because Sartre holds that man himself knows a priori that he is trying to be God of his own being. It is actually based on the experience of the enormous freedom of man which motivates him to be God of himself.

> A priori does not mean prior to experience in Sartre's philosophy. But it is not related to any specific experience. The a priori here, has nothing to do with any sort of constitutive principal which are prior to experience. It relates to a universality and necessity which are contained in every experience but which transcends any particulars experience.[18]

The experience on which Sartre depends is experience of whole human life, not a single experience but an experience of the whole human life.

This method of a priori description can reconcile between the subjective and objective interpretation of human reality. Inductive interpretation of Sartre's concept of human aspiration creates a distance between particular and universal. In induction, universal gives a new knowledge, which is not there in particular. There seems to be no such difference is Sartre's philosophy between "particular project" and "universal purpose". Every particular project or individual project can be judged as to have that universal purpose. In induction there is no way to judge the universality in every individual project.

Thus by showing every individual project to have a universal purpose, Sartre is reconciling between subjective and objective interpretation of human reality. This reconciliation can be understood better in Sartre's concept of 'totality' which man aspires to achieve. Sartre discusses 'totality, as human destiny which is revealed as 'totalisation' through man's particular actions. Man aspires to have the 'totality' but surpasses it by his every action in order to avoid being relegated to a state of an object. Totality is not outside human action as it is manifested through human action. Totality gets expressed in 'parts'. Sartre, therefore, does not find any duality between 'parts' and the 'whole' rather finds them united. But this unity is a "synthetic unity" of the 'unified'. Sartre actually tries to show that if we have to believe in any dialectic between man and the world, it is the dialectic between the 'totalisation' and 'totality'. Man's particular actions are expressing nothing but the totality of the world. World's totality is manifested as totalisation that is by man's particular actions only. Sartre explicates that there is no way to conceive 'totality' without participating in it as he does not believe in a "contemplative grasp" of 'totality'.[19]

Manifestation of the totality, for Sartre, is nothing but

singularisation which he calls 'incarnation'. Thus it seems that, 'totalisation' cannot but appear as 'singularisation'. 'Incarnation' means 'totality' is 'individuated'. So in manifestation of the 'totality', the 'singularity' is maintained.

> ... in a synthetic unification, the part is totalisation of the whole, incarnation is an individual form of totalisation. And by this we do not mean that it is symbol of expression, but it realises itself in a very real and practical sense as *totality producing itself here and now*. Every boxing match incarnates the whole of the boxing as an incarnation of all fundamental violence.[20]

Sartre does not believe in any ontological and logical difference between 'totalisation' and 'incarnation'. We have pointed out that Sartre does not believe in "contemplative grasp" or conceptual understanding of totality. He believes in the "critical experience"[21] of totality which can only be achieved by direct or indirect participation. Thus the experience of "fundamental violence" through every particular match of boxing cannot be witnessing the violence but participating in it directly or indirectly. Sartre believes that the boxers of the match and the viewers of the match are participating in the totality of the violence or the fundamental violence.[22] Sartre made it clear that singular events are not contingent events and totality is not necessary event. Like analytic reason Sartre does not consider "fundamental violence" as universal whose every specification is contingent.[23]

Though totalisation of violence is effected by each of the gesture of the participants of boxing but it is not a project with self awareness.[24] Thus Sartre holds that singularity is accidental and under no circumstance it can be conceptualised.[25] Sartre points out how singular events are undetermined and overflow themselves.

> The fundamental violence explodes here and now, but with all the features of here and now: in other

> words with opaque richness of the concrete and negative determination.[26]

It seems that every singular project preserves and transcends their singularity at a time in manifesting the totality. This is what Sartre calls "totalization" of "envelopment"[27] which implies "the integration of all concrete individual by praxis.[28] Every singular project 'envelops' totalisation as singularity; thus it is a negative determination of totality. The idea of 'envelopment' of totality by singular project seems to strengthen the impossibility of the conceptualisation of the 'totality' for their opacity and richness. They are opaque as they are expressing the totality as impenetrable. They are rich as they overflow themselves by manifesting the whole and not being confined to any singularity. Actions are singular they are, no way determined by the whole but are manifesting the whole. Sartre describes this 'envelopment' as a historical process. Sartre seems to conceive this 'envelopment' in the international historical context. Even he finds individuation of international movement as necessary. Otherwise, Sartre thinks, man will be isolated and will face 'idiosyncrasy' of impotence and failure. Thus Sartre finds man to mediate between society and sovereign individuality.

> the particular boxing match takes place in a climate of international tension ...[29]

Sartre feels the necessity of human action to manifest a totality of human reality. He does not accept any action as an isolated one. He accepts the individuality of action with its possibility to manifest the totality. It cannot manifest it at a time, due to its individuality which is always with the anguish of loosing it.

The Spiral of Human Action

The anguish of loosing individuality and the possibility of manifesting the totality makes human action circular. Action begins as an individual action, manifesting nothing but a totality but with the anguish of loosing individuality, so turn back to itself. Thus human action becomes circular. It occurs again to project his individuality, it manifests totality and again turns back to its individuality. The human action becomes spiral for this perpetuity. Circularity which reveals the totalisation never completes the 'circle in order to keep individuality, and human action becomes a spiral.[30] The question is how man's action forms a 'circularity'. Totality which man's actions manifest is the practical field of man's action in which it takes place. It is nothing but the socio-political world.

> ... one is moving from men to their practical field through praxis and only to return from practical field to men....[31]

Thus every expression of 'totality' turns back to the particularity again. Thus it forms a circle without completion and it is due to the perpetuity of the particular actions. Every time it starts from particular point overflows itself as it is to reveal the totality the whole but cannot reveal it at a time, occur again and again as an endless process and forms a 'spiral'. This 'spiral' indicates how particular and global or universal events are woven in a same thread. If we consider the particular events as subjective events, totality or the universality will be the objective side of it. We can say that it is objective truth of violence is getting expressed through the individuals boxing etc. Thus every subjective project contains objectivity and every objective truth is expressed as subjective action or event. The reconciliation between subjectivity and objectivity is peculiar to hermeneutic interpretation, of course without the spiraled form. The reconciliation between subjective condition and objective understanding we find in the interpretation of history and "life world" by hermeneutic philosophers. So before discussing Sartre's experiential interpretation of human aspiration which is actually operative in "socio-historical world". We would like to focus on the thought of hermeneutic philosophers about history and "life world" in our next chapter.

References

1. BN., pp. 612-614.
2. BN., p. 615.
3. PM., pp. 91-92.
4. BN., p. 618.
5. EH., p. 43.
6. BN., pp. 723-724.
7. *Ibid.*, p. 789.
8. *Ibid.*, p. 616.
9. Situation III, pp. 205-206.
10. BN., pp. 707-710.
11. BN., p. 616.
12. *Ibid.*, p. 616.
13. EH., pp. 45-46.
14. EH., p. 42.
15. Barbone S. Nothingness and Sartre's Fundamental Project Philosophy Today, Vol. 38, No.2 Summer '94 pp. 191-200.
16. PM., p. 108.
17. PM., p. 106.
18. CDRI, p. 35.
19. CDR. Vol. I, "The dialectic as the living logic of action is invisible to a contemplative reason – appears in course of praxis as a necessary moment of it", pp. 421-24.
20. CDR II, p. 77.
21. CDR I, p. 424.
22. CDR II (we should note that totality and fundamental has the same significance in Sartre's philosophy), p. 30.
23. CDR II, pp. 24-35.
29. *Ibid.*, p. 188.
30. *Ibid.*, p. 236.
31. *Ibid.*, p. 237.

References

4

Hermeneutics - Reconciliation between Subjectivity and Objectivity

In the previous chapters we have tried to develop Sartre's method as reconciliation between subjectivity and objectivity. Sartre neither accepts Husserl's "transcendental ego" as an "apodectic evidence" for the essential knowledge of things nor he considers being like Heidegger as prior to consciousness which illuminates it. Rather for him being and consciousness are 'contemporaneous'. Further, we have tried to show that Sartre's method interprets human aspiration and starts with man's 'situation' which is "given in perception". But empirical observation of man's individual project which is directed towards the world for individual purpose, cannot give us the idea of "fundamental project" of man. It cannot find both subjective and universal purpose in every particular project except the particular purpose for which it is taken. Inductive inference being a method based on empirical observation of particulars appears to bear some similarity with Sartre's method since "fundamental project" is actually designed by "particular project". But inductive inference as we have discussed, cannot necessarily consider every particular to be the expression of the universal. The particular projects are conceptualised by Sartre as the necessary expression of "universal purpose" or "fundamental project".

Sartre maintains this necessity in considering every single boxing match as incarnation of totality of violence. But the victory is singular. It can be argued that when both the boxers are participating in the totalisation of violence and one of them wins, the question arises, can one say this victory is an incarnation of the totality of violence? Can we say that the defeated is equally participating in the total process? Sartre admits that victory is singular as a "final moment of temporalisation". But the facticity of this victory, for Sartre, is necessarily rerated to the fundamental facticity of violence. However singular the victory may be, it cannot be simply contingent. The facticity that is the situation or condition which is given to any violence that is to conquer over the other or to dominate or get rid of other is the fundamental or the total situation given to the totality of violence.

> Victory of course – as a final moment of temporalisation – is singuiar : it appears as a unique and dated event manifesting its contingency rather than its necessity. But also no one is crazy enough to expect it to appear with the abstract harshness... The human event is at once contingent and necessary. Its facticity - product of the fundamental facticity of historical agents can be defined as the necessity of its contingency.[1]

We can say that any victory of a violent event is contingent but necessarily related to the totality of the violence.

But obviously Sartre does not believe that we can derive the "singular project" from the "total project". Therefore, Sartre's method cannot be considered as deductive either'. At the same time, the situation, in which man takes his "particular project" as a revelation of the very "fundamental project", is a socio-historical world. This world is a place of reconciliation between subjectivity and objectivity of human project. History is the result or the outcome of the man world interaction. We have discussed in our previous chapters how we are objectified by other and how our "fundamental project" of being" an "unique person", the "self cause" actually the effort to surpass the "objectification" imposed by the mere presence of 'other'. The world history is a record of such man to man interaction.

History – A Context not a Condition

In our first chapter we have discussed Sartre's views where he holds that man does not want to grasp the being of the world as his being but when he finds the world too difficult to grasp (as in its perception it is related to diverse aspects which makes man's life a ceaseless effort to grasp the world as a "quality of things") he tries to change the world. But we don't find men to be successful in his effort, since man himself in Sartre's philosophy, being characterised as consciousness, is responsible for the world to be ceaseless appearance in profiles and supersedes any knowledge we can have about the world. George Lichtheim[2] seems to find such explanation of. Sartre as an example of French movement in literature in post war situation. As history cannot be rewritten, the situation which is given to us cannot be changed Sartre's philosophy as well as the whole of French philosophy is a result of 'failure', in according with Lichtheim. Lichtheim finds Sartre to unite thoughts of Hegel, Marx and Heidegger, in his thought. In *Being and Nothingness* Lichtheim finds Sartre neglecting the social existence of man which is highlighted in *Critique*. In *Problem of Method* he finds Sartre to explicate social existence as a "group behaviour" and history as a 'disclosure' of truth of man in terms of his place in history which gives a picture of human situation in 'totality'. He finds it as reassertion of Hegel's philosophy. He finds Sartre accepting "intellectual understanding" of the world where reason indicates a "complex arrangement" to produce an "order of being" and Sartre is accepting the dialectical reason of Hegel and Marx but opposes neo-Marxist. But with the help of the distinction between Hegel and Kierkegaard made by G. Schrader, we can bring out the difference between Hegel and Sartre.

In George Schrader's word, Hegel's rationalistic explanation of world is a belief in a 'spirit' which constitutes the dialectics of man's being as alienated from him. Man exists not for himself but for others. Thus Hegel sees man as dominated by intellectual understanding of the world history. Hegel finds each step of dialectic to be dictated by what has gone before and what is yet to happen. Schrader pointed out Kierkegaard's opposition to Hegel. Kierkegaard believed that individual action are not motivated by "reason" but by "passion".[3] It appeals that Sartre's anguish against neo-Marxist which has been pointed out by Lichtheim, can equally go against Hegel. On the basis of Lichtheim and Schrader's interpretation, we can say that Sartre considers Hegel as well as neo-Marxist to be wrong to reduce any event or any individual action to a few general concepts. Sartre argues against marx that Marx views "individual epoche" as being shaped by "socio-economic" circumstances of the state but it is actually to break the circumstances. Sartre believes that any human action is to surpass or overcome the present situation. He gave example that in capitalist countries, all possible groups of the society surpass capitalism through their actions. Labour class concentrates in accumulating food and essential commodities, whereas aristocrats concentrate on cultural requirement. For Sartre, the actions of both the groups come out from the same economic situation but both are surpassing the situation into different direction. Even those who are busy in accumulation of money, they too are trying to surpass the present situation.

Lichtheim interprets after Sartre that the "practico inerte" indicates man's failure to comprehend himself in a society which indicates his existence to have a bond with other in need, in an atmosphere of scarcity. This bond is not a congenial bond since men are pitted against each other. Lichtheim holds that Sartre is at his best when he deals with individuals and not with history. Lichtheim seems to be right in interpreting Sartre in opposing the belief that a socio-economic situation determines man's individual action. We find Sartre in *Problem of Method* in opposing "idealist

Marxist" view according to which socio-economic situation is a "principle of inertia" of which man is a "passive product".

> ... Marxism had reabsorbed man into the idea, and existentialism seeks him everywhere where he is ... Idealist Marxism seems to have chosen the easiest interpretation; entirely determined by prior circumstances – that is - by economic conditions - man is a passive product, a sum of conditioned reflexes – it changes society in the way that a bomb, without ceasing to obey the principle of inertia can destroy a building.[4]

Sartre believes that full understanding of Marxism implies that man cannot simply be a product of prior condition as history can supersede man because history is not made up of a single man's activity but "men in plural". Man gets the result of his action as a "totalising movement" thus gets alienated in history. History is a "foreign force" but not isolated since man is making history.[5] Lichtheim seems to be wrong in thinking that Sartre is considering individuality as opposed to history. Rather for Sartre man is 'objectified' in history because the result of his action is not in him but in the 'totalisation' which is there in the external world. History is out of his reach but made up of his action only. Sartre considers history not only as a 'situation' in which man acts but it is also the 'future' of man because as "totalised movement" it can effect to back the single man.

> ... it is not true that history appears to us as an entirely alien force, each day with our own hands we make it something other than that what we believe we are making it, and history, backfiring, makes us other than we believe ourselves to be....[6]

It seems then that history is a source of reconciliation between subjectivity and objectivity of man's "situation" since we make history and history makes us. In the next chapter we will try to develop the historical moorings of the post war situation for the concept of 'nothingness' of Sartre.

Human situation is discussed by relating man to history, in hermeneutical philosophy. Therefore, in this chapter we will discuss the way history is considered as reconciliation between subjectivity and objectivity by the hermeneutic philosophers.

History in Hermeneutics

Hermeneutics as a whole develops a method of interpretation with the awareness of one's own history as well as of mankind. For hermeneutic philosopher awareness of other's emotional state is a precondition to judge our action towards other. And we have to reconstruct the inner life of other through self-understanding.

In our preceding chapters, we have tried to show Sartre's method to reconcile between the subjectivity and objectivity of human situation, he does so since he believes in a "circular dialectic" of human reality in the world of objects as well as in the world of others.

> "Man is mediated by things to the same extent things are mediated by man?[7]

Similarly, man in his "being-for-other" is influenced by 'Other' and influence 'Other' to the same extent. 'Other' causes a limitation to his "freedom" since man exercises his "freedom" upon 'Other'. So the world is considered by Sartre as being made up of things and 'Other' as an objectivity which man has to counter as subjectivity. Thus, before discussing such interpretation of human situation by Sartre which he does actually by the mediation of Socio-historical world, we can discuss some of the basic idea of hermeneutical philosophers and later we like to point out Sartre's method as similar to the hermeneutical method of interpretation to some extent as he reconciles between subjectivity and objectivity of human situation.

Dilthey agrees with the view of Locke, Hume and Kant that philosophy is founded on the fact of consciousness but differs from them as they consider consciousness simply to be the knowing subject. Dilthey considers consciousness as identical with the whole man as revealed by the linguistic and historical experience which reveals the relationship of one with other. This can be grasped not by "rigid a priori", principle of cognitive faculty, but by studying the totality of his being by observing the course of development of man himself and other. For this Dilthey adopts the method of experience which is not limited to some place or to sometime but goes as a process.

> It will deduce the real principle of knowledge in the human studies step by step from experience - mind discovers itself on higher and higher levels of systematic connection — of mind in the I in the thou, in every subject within a community....[8]

Through the above procedure, Dilthey believes one can study the objectivity of the subject's consciousness, but he expresses doubt whether this objectivity which consists in the system of a community is identical with the generality of individual mind's expression.

> If by this procedure we come to recognise the objectivity of the world of mind built up in the subject consciousness. We must then go on to ask how much this can contribute to the problem of knowledge in general.[9]

Dilthey does not find objectivity or community identical with generality, an individual studied in the context of a community gives an objective understanding and neither subjective nor general.

For Dilthey, life is a stream of process which is 'temporal'. It is a varied succession in which Dilthey finds 'uniformity'. In this temporal flow of life each moment becomes 'past', becomes 'crystallised' and 'preserved' and gradually gets a permanent forms. This preserved and crystallised part is the objectivity of man's life. Thus a lived or spent up experience understands life.

> The whole life is a structural system of lived experience.[10]

Dilthey finds mind to play a crucial role in this understanding. He notices a cause – effect relation among different attitudes of mind. For Dilthey "image" is formed by "senses" and causes a "satisfaction" or feeling of "fulfillment" which causes further will and action. For Sartre too it seems that 'image' gives a satisfaction since object is grasped in its entirety. Similarly, Sartre finds image to take its elements from perceptual world or the "world of reality". We also find that in this image, the object posited by consciousness is "absent in actuality", so can never be grasped in its "actuality", thus it can be the cause for consciousness to remain as a process throughout its existence. Dilthey holds further that the image which is formed by senses and combined with 'satisfaction' causes the structural system of our memory which causes further action. For Dilthey we know the force of action only from the "lived experience" and not by inferring a cause from action. "Understanding" for Dilthey, is always of some individual fact. Through induction we can have a systematic connection between work and person and can get a general human nature. But for Dilthey, both objective mind that is the "preserved" "structure" of "memory" and the individual power determine the world of mind. In induction for Dilthey, we understand individuals by virtue of their affinity with one another. Induction presupposes the relation between the multiple mental expressions and presupposes a general human nature. Thus though induction takes place by collecting individual data, the presupposition of it makes the business of understanding an endless process by taking a more and more developed forms of mental expression and penetrating into ever greater depth of the "mind-constructed-world". Sartre too will agree that from the empirical observation of the world phenomena and human activity, we cannot induce the human reality which signifies a 'lack'. Induction itself is an indefinite method. In perception the world appears with its infiniteness and cannot get the world in its entirety in finite time perception transcends itself to imagination to form an image of object in its entirety. Sartre too along with Dilthey does not believe in a generality of human nature since he believes that "particular projects" are accidental. There is every possibility of giving up a "particular project". So the "global project" so which is manifested through the particular project remains undetermined.

The presupposition, with which hermeneutics deals, is that every singular expression of life can be interpreted by raising it to the level of objectivity which is the preserved memory or history in Diltheyian interpretation. It is only from the preserved memory of past humanity, man takes the power for further action. But such understanding of singular objectivity cannot ensure a universal validity, since there is always a contrast between the singular expression and the knowledge of man's nature.

> "... manifestation of my nature which has appeared in the sensible world confronts me like that of a stranger, and that as such I am unable to interpret it, or in the other case that I have got into a state which I stare at as if it were someone else's ... Inner experience in which l become aware of my own state, can never by itself make conscious of my own individuality. It is only by comparing myself with other that I come to experience what is individual in myself..."[11]

From this we can conclude that the objectivity of man considered by Sartre as well as Dilthey is more or less the same. For both of them man's individuality is an objectified individuality by the world. Both seem to consider objectified nature of man to be the only possibility of man. But the objectivity in no way limits the subjectivity of man. The outstanding feature of Dilthey's philosophy is the consideration of objectivity as a preserved memory and as a power of man's action which we don't find in Sartre's philosophy, in the same sense.

Dithey's view can be summed up as follows: the sensible world can supply us the objectivity of mental expression as a preserved memory of humanity from which man can acquire power and go for further action. But this objectivity is not the generality of the mental expression. Thus the method which presupposes generality cannot successfully bring out a human nature. There is no other way to understand individual mental expression without comparing it with the objectivity of mental expression, though the sole 'understandable' is the individual. For Sartre, objectivity is imposed upon man by other or by the system of the world what man chooses to follow. But this objectification provokes man for action. Unlike Dilthey, Sartre holds that man's further action aims to overcome objectivity imposed by the world or 'other' and to maintain its subjectivity. Dilthey has not discussed any such negation of objectivity in his philosophy. But, for both Dilthey and Sartre, individual subjective actions are independent of the objectivity as such.

In Dilthey we find that individual actions appear in the world as being objectified which works as a "preserved memory" which provides power to the acting man. Ricoeur finds this objectivity as history, as "worked out" 'past'.

> ... the objectivity is what thought has worked out, put into order, understood – hence we expect history to make the past of human societies attain the dignity of objectivity.[12]

We find Ricoeur to discuss subjectivity from two angles, one from the angle of the historian and the other from the angle of philosophers in relation to history. A historian crafts history and a philosopher reads history. Historian's subjectivity consists in the understanding of history as a completed form of movement of man's thought and action on the whole. Historian has no right to 'denominate' historical event according to his wish. If it is to determine the structure, historian cannot determine. Historian can study that which is present before him in its past as it was, as a memory, and its future as it was at that time.

> "The historian is never in the position of mathematicians who denominates and determines the structure of a notion: On the other hand, historian considers the epoche that, he studies of present reference. Such a present has future of that time and not of the thing which we know happened. That present also has a past – not of what we know their past. Now this projection into another present which belongs to the type of objectivity proper to history is a kind of *imagination* is certain that this imagination is the mark of subjectivity.[13]

Thus Ricoeur's concept of objectivity is not like Sartre or Dilthey which surpasses subjectivity. Objectification of subjectivity of Ricoeur is the reflection of subjectivity itself in the form of imagination. But we should notice that for Ricoeur the subject has no scope to imagine apart from the actual past. Thus the claim of imagination of Ricoeur is weakened by this.

But Ricoeur also holds that by considering the past and present historical events, historian is fabricating a "causal network" of other's or past-men's action. Here he seems to use his imagination.

> ... we meet up with the problem of integral past, for what the historians attempt, to restore through the whole network of causal relations, is precisely what other men have experienced.[14]

Thus Ricoeur thinks that history is also 'encountered' as well as 'explained' by the historian.

> History, therefore, is animated by a will for *encounter* as much as by a will for explanation.[15]

He holds that when a historian considers some past to some present as a "memory of past men", historian gives value to this memory. He is not only interested in those values but he is close to the task of contemporary person which he cannot 'relive'.

> The historian goes to the men of past with his own human experience – history makes the values of past men – this calling up of values – the only way of evoking that is open to us since we are unable to relive what they lived – it is not possible unless historians are vitally "interested" in those values and have a deep affinity for the task.[16]

Thus that objectivity of history which the historian deals with is an objectivity chosen by the subject. It is based on the subject's 'interest' in the value of "past men". It seems similar to Sartre's concept of objectivity, since for Sartre, the objectivity is actually chosen by the freedom of man himself. Ricoeur explains that this subjectivity is not the historian's subjectivity rather it is the subjectivity of history only. This view is also similar to Sartre since Sartre holds that though history is made up of man but not by a single man but by "men in plural" it supersedes individual. Ricoeur also holds that in historical understanding, historian brings out past men's subjectivity by suppressing his own subjectivity.

> ... the objectivity of history brings out the latent subjectivity of history and no longer just the historian's subjectivity.[17]

In this regard Ricoeur distinguishes between "good subjectivity" and "bad subjectivity". A "good subjectivity" is compatible with the subjectivity of history. It is that subjectivity which is not simply personal but a subjectivity of mankind.

Another stand point from which Ricoeur tried to explicate the nature of subjectivity is the subjectivity of a philosopher. Philosopher is a reader of history for Ricoeur but not in the simple sense. Rather, philosopher discovers the fact of history as he reflects history to be.

> The philosopher may make of the historian's history. The philosopher has a specific way of fulfilling historian's work. This consists in making his own "self discovery" coincides with a 'recovery' of history.[18]

Philosopher wants to get the justification of his thought in the context of history. There are two-fold presuppositions behind the 'expectation' for Ricoeur – one is the systematic coherent history, every event of which is followed from another; two, history develops as man develops i.e. through the promotion of values. Thus, according to Ricoeur, philosopher rejects those facts which are "exceptional", "non-systematisable" and "individual". Ricoeur holds at the same time that historical understanding is an understanding of a movement as a whole. Thus Ricoeur finds that historian's world is more open than that of the philosopher the latter tries to categories history to get a coherent order in history.

It is noticeable that while considering the "past" events historian is considering some "value" as the "only way of evoking man" and reflects his own value in his depiction. History is a "series of disconnected appearances" each of which has to be 'encountered' separately and a new which are irreducible to generality. Recoeur, therefore, talks about some latent paradox between "history in a singular" and "man in plural". The former is the expectation of rationalist philosophers, for Ricoeur, to have a unified human meaning. But the latter is the subject matter of the historians who define history as a science of "past men" which implies history to be of manifold expressions of men. But to have "good subjectivity,' for Ricoeur, one has to regard history, as a process goes from "man to mankind". Existential philosophers, for Ricoeur', can reconcile between man and mankind by recognising cosmos to be an exceptional centre of existence which expresses "manifolds" of man's movement and the "thought" which expresses the "movement as a whole.

To sum up Ricoeur's discussion, we can say that history is the "past movement" understood and conceived as a "whole". The understanding of history by present man, either by a historian or a philosopher, reflects history as their own value; thus justifies their own value in the context of history. It seems that Ricoeur finds the objectivity of man's action in the form of history as an ideal of man, consists in a process which moves from individual to mass. But to interpret Ricoeur's thought from Sartrean stand point it seems that since there is no way to "denominate" history by the subject, history appears in "opacity" to man. Similarly, in Sartrean philosophy we find history to appear as an objectivity of man but it is also an end of man and at the same time it surpasses man as it is an expression of "men in plural". It seems that the "paradox" Ricoeur talks about, if we try to interpret it in Sartrean perspective, we will find it as a "paradox" between the single subjective angle taken on history and the history as a movement as a 'whole'. It is paradoxical in Ricoeur's philosophy that on the one hand, historians or philosophers can interpret history on the basis of affinity or reflection of their own value in history, but on the other hand, history surpasses their subjectivity. One is considering history as a movement of mankind. Another brings out a coherent system out of it. But both of them have to deal with mankind despite their subjective angle which they take on history, they are objectified in historical understanding. This paradox in Sartre's philosophy will be discussed in the next chapter.

In Habermas's concept of "life world" we find this subject-object reconciliation. "Life world" for him has a two-fold meaning, it is the 'context' of culture, society and personality, and it is the 'resource' or possibility from which man can transmit and renew cultural knowledge. It gives him a social identity and at the same time the 'solidarity.[19] The "life world", for Habermas, should be understood in terms of both action and "material subtratum" of society. It seems that for him "life world" indicates both movement of society and a context which stimulates and preserves movement. Social existence for Habermas is not only characterised by the 'intention' of social agent or man but also by a context which generates action and at the same time indicates 'extent' for action in terms of 'recognition' and 'realisation' of 'intention'.[20]

"Life world" for Habermas offers a commonly accepted background of knowledge in which action can be 'coordinated'. It is not only cultural tradition 'of community'. It promotes three kinds of "performative actions" in men, in their "communicative action". First the action objectifies outside world by surpassing the existing culture; second, it surpasses by setting a standard; third, it expresses thus an "inner subjectivity".[21] By ascribing such totality to the "life world" Habermas expresses a movement of it that advances towards a better society. Thus Habermas considers "life world" as a universal history. The "universal history" that the life world indicates is not only an "inventory" of past or present culture but an objective 'complement' or 'recognition' of subjective or inter subjective action and intention. By comparing the concept of history of Habermas with that of Sartre, it seems though Habermas considered "life world" as a "universal human history" in which human actions are preserved, but Sartre will refuse to consider "life world" as a "material subtratum" of action. But like Habermas, Sartre finds it to be the objectification of particular men which he tries to surpass by considering it an alien world. Though Sartre finds history to be made up of man's action but sees it as an "objectification" of man's action since it is actually made up of "men in plural" and the result of man's action surpasses man's expectation. Though Sartre like Habermas finds "life world" or history to be the possibility, recognition, and "complement" but for Sartre it is not equal to man's expectation. Habermas does not find history to create any 'lack' which men would surpass. It is only for the betterment of human action and society man surpasses history. But no betterment is explicitly considered in Sartre's philosophy as the cause for surpassing history. Moreover, Sartre does not find history to be universal because he believes in constant making of history. The universality of history is "narrowed down" in his philosophy. But both Sartre and Habermas considers history to be the expression of 'intersubjectivity' in terms of complement and recognition. We will discuss in our next chapter how social historical world in the form of 'intersubjectivity', without having a universality of human action, creates lack in man which man tries to surpass in its every action. Unlike Habermas Sartre holds that the human situation which man tries to surpass is made up of human action only.

Another hermeneutic philosopher Hans George Gadamar[22], the philosophy of whom contains some Hegelian elements in its concept of history with which Sartre does not agree, but the hermeneutical effort to reconcile between subjective and objective understanding of human situation, is the point we want to highlight here. Hermeneutical understanding of history does not mean to have an objective knowledge of history. Rather it seems that understanding of history is necessitated by the hermeneutical understanding of consciousness. We can start discussing Gadamar's notion of history by considering two things which he holds about history. First the understanding of history should consider it to be an "effective history" and second, this understanding is in fact an infinite process (The concept of effective history indicates that we are not outside history, so we cannot have an objective knowledge of history but can consider a part of it, in which we are, as whole). The reason Gadamar upholds for this infinite process is based on that which is "historically pre-given". All subjective understanding of our own situation are determined by the 'substance' history.[23] We have noticed by comparing Habermas and Sartre that for both of them history cannot be a determinant 'substance' which can't determine human action but can make action as an objectivity which is to be surpassed.

For Gadamar the understanding of history is limited to the particular concept of the situation, in contrast with the 'horizon' which is the essential part of this concept which includes everything that every particular situation can have. There can be historical understanding of 'horizon' by excluding particular horizon not in terms of "contemporary criteria" of the past. Gadamar's historical consciousness places within itself the historical 'horizon' which does not mean that consciousness has to go to an isolated alien world which has no connection with its own. Rather the great horizon originates from within and goes beyond the "frontiers of the present"[24]. It seems to be a single "horizon" that embraces everything which a historical consciousness can contain.[25] Not by placing itself into "historical horizon" that but by having it within itself. Consciousness should have it without having any 'disregard' for its own self. It cannot be acquired by the 'empathy' for other. Not even through the placing of our own criteria we can have it. It seems that "historical consciousness" of universality that can go beyond any particularity, is either the particularity of myself or of other.

A true "historical consciousness" seems to have the same view on both the situations either of one's own or of other. But it is not worthy that Gadamar seems to believe this "historical horizon" as a 'fusion' of present and past since in every encounter between present and past he finds a 'tension'. Every 'hope' and 'fear' of present for Gadamar is based on considering the past as a 'testimony'. This "tension" cannot be covered by a "naive assimilation" but by a 'fusion' which has to be brought out. It is not the case that past and present will be naturally absorbed into one another but by retaining their identity they can be mixed up. It seems that for Gadamar projecting of the "historical horizon" is a 'phase' in the process of understanding. So he does not find consciousness to be "solidified" into the "self alienation" of the consciousness of the past.

We may conclude that Gadamar conceived a necessary and infinite historical understanding of consciousness for which it must have a great vision or 'horizon'. Such consciousness can go beyond man's particular present, either of his own or of others but this 'horizon' is originated within the consciousness and takes itself within it. Thus consciousness does not lead to an 'alien' world. It can be acquired by a wide view on other's present as well as his own, it does not mean, 'empathy' for other not even a 'disregard' of one's own. This wide view indicates a universality that goes beyond particular situation. This unified view cannot cover the tension between the present and past. Past is the standard of justifying present 'hope' as well as 'fear', so these cannot be any natural assimilation. Thus it seems that "historical consciousness" is a rational' requirement of consciousness to gain an universal knowledge of the human action where there is an objective context, in which subjective actions are included but can be understood by going beyond the subjectivity.

Sartre differs from Gadamar since for Sartre the going beyond the present situation is not the requirement of consciousness rather it is the nature of consciousness. This going beyond of consciousness expresses the two dimensional characters in Sartre's philosophy which are "being-for-itself" and at the same time "being-for-other". The 'horizon' cannot be acquired for Gadamar by disregarding particular situation of our own. This view of Gadamar is similar to the view of Sartre. For Sartre's historical understanding of individual project are definitely the expression of human freedom and subjectivity. Gadamar, therefore, views "historical horizon" not as an 'alienation' or 'solidification' of present man but for Sartre despite the freedom of individual project, history appears to be an objectification of man, it is made up of 'men in plural' that supersedes individual man. But contrarily Gadamar holds that present action of man is conditioned by the history which is a 'substance' and a 'testimony' for the present action. Although the particular situation is included in the historical understanding of the 'horizon' but actually there is no freedom in man's particular situation in Gadamar's philosophy.

Sartre's concept of 'objectification' of man in history and the freedom of man's action express an original tension between man's action and the result he gets in history. In the next chapter we will focus on this tension which is actually the result of man's freedom. The socio-historical world does not fulfill the expectation of man with full equivalence, it is considered as the objectification of man.

References

1. CDR II, p. 77.
2. G. Lichtheim. *The Concept of Ideology and Other Essay*, pp. 289-315.
3. Schrader, G. Jr. (Editor), Existential Philosopher Mc-Grow-HIL Book C... N. Y. 1967, pp. 13-15 (Sartre too considers human action to be an expression of passion and emotion. So no prior or later situation to the action can – originate action).
4. PM., pp. 85-86.
5. PM., pp. 87-89.
6. PM., p. 90.
7. CDR I., p. 169.
8. Hodges H. A. Wilheim Dilthey. An introduction (to the task of a critique of historical reason, G.S. 191-192) Routledge & Kegan Paul itd Broadway House 1949. p. 114.
9. *Ibid.,* p. 114.
10. Wiltheim Dilthey – An Introduction, Hodges H.A., p. 116.
11. Wilheim Dilthey – An Introduction (excerpts 317-320 Introduction to the rise of Hermeneutics), pp. 125-126.
12. Ricoeur Paul. History and Truth. Trans with an Intro by C. Kelbley. N. W. Uni. Preis Evausion. 1965. p. 21.
13. History and Truth, Ricoeur, pp. 27-28.
14. *Ibid.,* p. 28.
15. *Ibid.,* p. 28.
16. *Ibid.,* p. 29.
17. *Ibid.,* p. 29.
18. History and Truth. Ricoeur, p. 32.
19. Habermas, Modernity and Law Ed by M. Defem, Sage Pholication 1998 p. 4.
20. *Ibid.,* p. 4.
21. *Ibid.,* p. 3.
22. Gadamar, H.G. Hermeneutic Reader. Ed by K. Muller-Vollmer. Basit Blackwell. 1985, pp. 268-269.
23. *Ibid.,* p. 269.
24. *Ibid.,* pp. 268-269.
25. *Ibid.,* p. 271.

5

The Hermeneutical Standpoint on Sartre

A Recap

From the understanding of the phenomenal world to the understanding of human reality we can see the effort of Sartre to reconcile between subjective and objective sides of understanding human reality. For Sartre every part of the appearance is given in the context of the whole, so the perception of the 'legs' is actually the perception of the legs of a chair. At the same time he thinks that the 'form' of the object which indicates the 'totality' is 'induced' as a 'future' perception on the basis of the successive perception of the present. In this induced future he does not see anything new than the present. But it seems that the 'totality' which cannot be grasped in the present, can be 'imagined' for Sartre. If Sartre's concept of imagination is interpreted as an induction it will not be a perfect one, the object posited by 'imagination' is not in perception but a new one as it is "absent in actuality". It is similar with the nature of the end posited in the 'fundamental project' of man. We have tried to interpret his method of conceiving human aspiration also as an induction. It seems that 'fundamental project', that is to have the primacy over the being of the 'for-itself' which is to have a hold over freedom of one's own as well as of other's, is induced from the perception of condemned human life and its paradoxical aspiration.

But the difficulty we had to face was that such interpretation would give rise to a duality between subjective and objective understanding of human nature, the reconciliation of which was an aim of Sartre. For Sartre there is actually no need to drive the 'fundamental projects' from the particular projects but through every 'particular project' 'the fundamental project is expressed'. By interpreting Sartre's philosophy as inductive inference we can only see the surpassing from one to another 'particular project' with particular ends but there in no way to judge them as an expression of a single 'fundamental project' because induction is based on the empirical observation which perhaps cannot judge the actual desire of every 'particular project'. And if we can interpret that from the known particular end, the unknown 'fundamental project' can be induced. Sartre would claim that we know the 'fundamental project' a priori that is without the basis of experience. But analysis of the method of Sartre in comparison to that of Husserl shows that while Husserl is 'bracketing' the experiential world for the 'essential' knowledge of the world on the basis of the 'reflective' consciousness which is a 'transcendental' 'evidence' of the knowledge, Sartre rejects the possibility of the reflection and phenomenological reduction and holds that consciousness is only a consciousness which is a 'pre-reflective' consciousness which is directed to the world and not to itself. There is no question of 'bracketing' the experiential world in Sartre's philosophy. Sartre is claiming that we have a priori knowledge of the 'fundamental project'. But Sartre may not be right in justifying his claim since he does not approach the knowledge of the fundamental end of man without the experiential world as a ground for it.

Inference from known ends to unknown ends is a kind of induction conceived by J.S. Mill.[1] But we have to keep Sartre's method free from any duality either between subjectivity and objectivity or between particular and universal; at the same time we have to keep the experiential connotation of his method which seems to be his point of departure from Husserl. Sartre clarifies his stand by saying that a priori description does not mean prior to experience.

> The "a priori" here has nothing to do with any sort of constitutive principles which are prior to experience. It relates to a universality and necessity which are contained in every experience but which transcends any particular experience.[2]

But Sartre does not believe in universality of human action from which particular action can be derived. We can say that universal human project has to be experienced. The question arises how can it be experienced in Sartrean frame work? In so far as universality of experience is concerned, we will find it to be an objective experience of the world which is not an isolated experience. But while retaining its singularity this experience is an individuality of totalisation.

> The subject-object duality, we can overcome by induction. Since there are some logicians who interpret induction as particulars considered on the basis of a universal idea.

But we will discuss rater in this chapter that no 'universality' at all is conceived by Sartre rather than the particular projects getting designed through the particular purpose, through the particular angle of apprehending the world. The apprehension of the world comes from the bi-polar experience of the world as both possibility and impossibility. This impossibility indicates either prohibitions or the affairs which are out of reach. It creates a 'lack' in men which he tries to overcome. All these interpretations seem to be based on Sartre's experience of the post war situation.

In this chapter, we will try to interpret Sartre's method as an experiential one by which he is trying to reconcile between subjective and objective understanding of man's action. Such method is mainly adopted by hermeneutic philosophers. Thus it becomes important to see under this interpretation whether Sartre's method is hermeneutical. We have already noticed in chapter IV that history is considered by hermeneutic philosophers as the source of the reconciliation between subjective human action and the objective understanding of it. On the one hand, history is made up of man's autonomous action; on the other, history influences human action by providing power or value or testimony. The difference we observed between Sartre and other hermeneutic philosophers is that, Sartre does not find history as something 'preserved'. History is rather a moving phenomenon for Sartre. It objectifies men, as it is made up of "men in plural". Differing from hermeneutic philosophers, Sartre does not find history to be simply a past rather it has a futuristic characteristic, as it objectifies and impels man for further action. Habermas's concept of history as 'complement' or 'recognition' bears some similarity with Sartre's concept of history. For Habermas also the human actions are to surpass "universal history" or "life world" for the betterment of human society. Sartre finds human action to originate out of scarcity or out of an 'antagonistic' relation among men. If any betterment can be conceived, it is a personal betterment. Whatever the world may be, man finds it to create a 'lack' in himself; so man tries to surpass it. Moreover, history is not a universality of man's action rather it is in constant reciprocation with the man by appearing as a source of 'lack' in man, so gets surpassed by human action and again becomes the source of 'lack'. The similarity we can see between Sartre and hermeneutic philosophers is the effort of reconciliation between subjectivity of man's action and the objectivity of man's action.

History of man's action seems to represent this reconciliation. This reconciliation is very much possible in Sartre's philosophy as he shows consciousness to bring 'nothingness' into the world as being directed infinitely towards the world and surpassing it infinitely. We can see how Sartre's concept of "social-historical-world" can be the situation for the reciprocation between the man and world to bring 'nothingness' into the world.

The Experiential Connotation

M. K. Bhadra points out that though the study of individual project in relation to 'fundamental project' is possible, but we do not have a clear consciousness of it. Thus he interprets this kind of philosophizing, as an hermeneutical effort of Sartre, as it considers any expression as the expression of that which is expressed.[3] It is true that Sartre is not saying that what he considers as 'fundamental project' is posited by consciousness explicitly.

But he considers all particular projects are the manifestation of the 'fundamental project'. Bhadra also pointed out that Sartre's method opposes the approach of Husserl since he does not find Husserl to be true enough to the experience.[4] It is presupposed that Sartre's method tries to be true to experience. But the question arises that: Is it possible to interpret every 'particular project' as to reveal the fundamental project on the basis of the experience of the 'existential world'? For this, the process in which 'nothingness' is brought into the world through consciousness, has to be experientially interpreted. 'Nothingness' implies the fact of the consciousness to reach object of the outer world which creates lack in consciousness which it tries to surpass. This surpassing is an infinite process, consciousness longs anxiously for the 'fundamental project' that is to have a being which can be at the onset of every action of man, so that man can get rid of his being reduced to action. The interpretation of Sartre's method as experiential finds the need to bring out the experiential background of Sartre's concept of 'nothingness'. We will try to do this what follows.

Being influenced by Romanticism, hermeneutics allows, for Carl Page, the "creative imagination" to trace the social-historical or cultural context for any human activity. Human situations are not described with reference to the fact it asserts or persuades to act in a specific manner. Carl Page in his article pointed out the detour interpretation of hermeneutics through the 'mediation' of history culture etc. which is rooted in dissatisfaction of the eighteenth century philosophers that is with the immediacy of sense perception as the only means of understanding. Scriptures, for example, are not immediately intelligible without understanding the social historical background.[5]

Sartre, by uniting all 'particular projects' as a manifestation of 'fundamental project', expresses a socio-political background of his thought. Carl Page is right in pointing out that human actions are not described with reference to what it asserts or persuades. It is applicable to Sartre's particular projects as they are not what they project but what manifest. But before going in that discussion, we should discuss hermeneutical effort of Sartre in which he considers the consciousness as a directedness to the world as a 'being-for-itself' and at the same time as a 'being-for-other'. In Droysen's hermeneutical thought human reality is essentially a 'totality' in itself and realises this totality by understanding others and being understood by others.[6]

Similarly, for Sartre, complete understanding of man is possible in his 'being-for-other'. It is the being of man that indicates the 'possibility' for which man 'lives'.

> .... I need the other in order to realise fully all the structure of my being.[7]

> .... the Other's existence was experienced with evidence in and through the fact of my objectivity – My reaction to my own alienation was expressed in my grasping the other as an object.[8]

> Similarly, for Sartre Other is not an object here and cannot be an object — unless by the same stroke myself ceases to be an object for-the-other....thus I do not aim at the Other as an object nor at my Ego as an object for myself: — I can be ashamed only as my freedom escapes me in order to become a given object.

> Shame reveals to me that I am this being, when I am

alone, I cannot realize my "being-seated":— But in order for me to be what I am, it suffices merely that the Other look at me.— Thus my possibility is present to my unreflective consciousness — I apprehend my possibility from outside....[9]

From the above discussion, it is clear that for Sartre my 'possibility' and 'situation' depends on my being an object-for-the-other as well as other's being an object-for-me.

From Sartre's discussion it follows that objectivity as well as the subjectivity cannot be understood as one to one relationship between me and other. It cannot be conceived either from my angle from the other's angle, but requires an over-all perspective capable of viewing the world and all men in it. It can only be a hermeneutical perspective. Thus Sartre's concept of objectivity, includes the whole world. By being the object of other's look, I find myself at the centre of the world from which it is the other who is at distance.

> .... the *Other's look* as the necessary condition of my objectivity is the destruction of all objectivity for me. The other's look touches me across the world and is not only a transformation of myself but a total metamorphosis of the 'world' I am looked-at-in a world which is looked-at.[10]

For Sartre man's possibility is neither a subjective possibility nor an objective possibility that is totally unrelated to one's own choice but a social possibility which is not identical to "individual possibility". Society gives a situation to man which is not an antecedent fact from which individual action can be derived but it is made up of men only. Man surpasses it, since it gives man his present possibility as being this or that and indicates his concreteness. Man tries to surpass it and goes towards the goal what he has chosen from the society only as his possibility.

> It is by transcending the given towards the field of possible and by realising one possibility from among all the others that the individual objectifies himself and contributes to making history.[11]

Socio-political Moorings of Nothingness

For Sartre, the understanding of human reality, in terms of possibility and situation is based on the social and historical objective situation of man and on the subjective choice of action. In a capitalist society, the situation of the workers motivates them to go beyond the hunger or poverty which is different from the "going beyond" of the upper class which is not centering itself in accumulating food etc, but for accumulating the cultural requirements. The shifting being of man which is characterised by "going beyond" implies 'nothingness' which is always to achieve something. Thus 'nothingness' seems to have a social meaning similar to 'need' and it seems to be analogous to the 'felt need' of the society in the post war situation.

> This going beyond we find at the very root of the human – in *need*. It is need which for example links the scarcity of women in Marquesas, as a structural fact of the group, — for this scarcity is not a simple lack: in its most naked form it expresses a situation in society and contains already an effort to go beyond it.[12]

'Lack' seems to be a personal feeling in which man finds himself as incomplete but 'need' implies already an effort to go beyond that situation. 'Need' is defined by Sartre as to explicate a total human reality.

> Everything is discoverable in need [besoin]; this is the first totalising relation between that material being, a man and the material group to which he belongs, This relation in *unilateral* is a relation of *interiority*. Through need as a matter of fact, there appears a matter, the first negation of negation and the first totalisation. Need is negation of negation to the extent that it expresses itself as a lack inside the organism:[13]

It is positivity to the extent that, through it the organic totality tends to conserve itself as such. The primitive negation is a first contradiction between the organic and the inorganic, in the double sense the lack defines itself for a totality. What is lacking can be reduced to unorganized or less organized elements, or simply to dead flesh, etc. From this point of view, the negation of this negation comes about by transcending the organic towards the inorganic.[14]

'Need' expresses the total human reality which lacks 'totality' in itself, and which is a drive to negate totality which is an organic totality. So what human action negates is already negated in himself. Need as negation of negation expresses the totality of the want of something inorganic or less organic. Thus need expresses a positivity. Similarly, 'nothingness' is not a negation. Let us come to the discussion of 'nothingness'.

Sartre explains need as the original tension in man and all efforts to bring a change in this world which seems to bring 'nothingness' into the world.

Without the original tension of need as a relation of interiority with nature there will be no change.[15]

> ....once there has been a change in economic. Cultural and effective relation among men, it will begin with the eradication of – material scarcity – the root of antagonism, past and present among men.[16]

Man exists for every one as non human man, as an alien species.... The mere existence of everyone is defined by the scarcity as the constant danger of non-existence.[17]

Here it is clear that for Sartre, non-existence or nothingness is brought into the world through man's action originated out of need.

> ... the whole human development at least upto now has been a bitter struggle against scarcity.[18]

Sartre's concept of 'nothingness' seems to be originated from man's scarcity and need. Scarcity is similar to 'lack' which man finds in him and also outside himself that is in the world. Need implies the effort of man to restore what man lacks. But for Sartre this scarcity is originated out of antagonism among men as well as it originates antagonism.

> The origin of struggle always lies, in fact, in some concrete antagonism whose material condition is scarcity – each refuses to serve the other's end, while recognising his objective being as means within the adversary's project. He uses his own instrumentality in other's to make them an instrument of his own ends.....[19]

We could say that scarcity and antagonism among men are in the same cycle of human struggle where everyone is making other an instrument of his end. So the scarcity for man himself and the way of overcoming it are factors for reducing man into a non human being. This socio historical behaviour of man seems to be the background of Sartre's concept of nothingness as a human reality.

Nothingness –As Subject-Object Reconciliation

We could discuss 'nothingness' as it is discovered by man with the mode of negation which is actually negation of negation in his relation to the world. Man for Sartre is related to the world in terms of questioning. Questioning is always accompanied by an expectation of a reply. World or being is supposed to answer this question in affirmative, since it is characterised as positivity. We get negative reply, for example, I want to see Pierre in a cafe, but the cafe or the world in which I want to find Pierre, gives a negative reply that Pierre is not here. The café does not express any negativity; it is "full positivity". But without being able to find Pierre in it, it is I who attribute negation to it. In this way I am expressing my situation in relation to the expectation of seeing Pierre. It expresses that my expectation is unfulfilled. Sartre made it clear that though consciousness brings 'nothingness' by the mode of 'negation' but it is not producing the 'negation; rather Sartre finds "consciousness" to experience negation. Consciousness of "negation" is a consciousness for that 'moment'. Thus 'negation' is neither subjective nor can be derived from the objective situation of the café. Is a real event, 'happens' between world and the expectation of the consciousness for certain element to see or have in it.

> I myself expected to see Pierre and my expectation has caused the absence of Pierre and to *happen* as a real event concerning this cafe. —Consciousness, moreover, cannot produce a negation except in the form of consciousness of negation.[20]

This 'nothingness comes into the world through the human reality by ascribing 'negation' to the world as a result of its unfulfilled expectation. It is neither subjective nor objective since 'nothingness' is the single expression used by Sartre for both the expectation of the subject for certain thing in the world and the non-fulfillment of that expectation which ascribes negation to that particular objective situation of the world.

> ... by a double movement of nihilation he nihilates the thing questioned in relation to itself by placing it in a neutral state, between being and non-being —and that he nihilates himself from the being in order to be able to bring out of himself the possibility of a non-being.[21]

The concept of 'nothingness' is related to human expectation. If one nihilates a thing, he places the thing between the state of being and non-being. It seems that the thing is placed between the fulfillment of the expectation and the non-fulfillment of the expectation. Nihilating act consists in separating man from both fulfillment and non-fulfillment. 'Being' is fulfillment for the 'non- being' consciousness. The nihilating act of man at first separates himself from the self, from the non-fulfillment, attaches itself to the possible fulfillment in the world. If the reply from the world is negative, man is separating himself from this non-fulfillment too and nihilates it again. Thus by double negation man brings 'nothingness' into the world. Thus 'Nothingness' indicates both subjectivity and objectivity of human existence.

Sartre's concept of 'nausea' boredom etc. can explicate this reconciliation between subjectivity and objectivity. For Sartre any description one can make about the world, is his interpretation of the event in which both he and the 'world' participate equally.

> ... there is nothing— you exaggerate everything, you are on the look out, and you continually stretch the truth — I can no longer write anything definite about — I am already too far away from it: all that I can say is that in neither case was there anything people world ordinarily call an event.[22]

From the above quotation it should not be interpreted about Sartre's philosophy that events are subject's mental construction. We should note the word 'exaggeration' indicates something to exist first in order to be exaggerated. But Sartre does not believe in any objectivity or existence devoid of subjectivity. The objectivity is revealed through and as the subjectivity only. So Sartre does not believe in "people world". The objective concern of subjectivity is also difficult to be traced out since it is nihilated by consciousness. So the objective concern is simply a pretention for Sartre.

So much for the exterior what happen inside me do not lrave any real traces. There was something which I saw and which disgusted me. But I no longer know whether I was looking at the sea or at the pebbles.—Any how it's certain that I was frightened or experienced some... lf only I knew what I was frightened of, I should have already made considerable progress. The odd thing is that I am not at all prepared to consider myself insane, I can see that I am not: all these changes concern objects. At least, that is what I would like to be sure about.[23]

Due to the subject object non-duality and nihilating mode of objective concern of man, it is hard to distinguish between the subjective concern and the object of the concern. Being frightened etc: are subjective experience but there must be an objective cause for it, otherwise it will indicate insanity. Though one cannot be sure about the objective fact of the fear, there is no way to differentiate objectivity from the subjective experience.

> There is something new, for example, about my hands, a certain way of picking my pipe or fork, or else it is the fork which now has a certain way of getting itself picked up.[24]

Thus it seems that the 'fork' or the object of external world has definitely a part in the emotion occurring, in the subject man. Though we find Rocquentin to see some emotional change in him about his feeling for the Autodidact but here he does not leave world as not to play any part in it.

> When the Autodidact came to say good morning to me, then there was his hand like a fat maggot in my hand. I let go it straight away; the hand fell back limply – I think it is I who has changed. But I have to admit that I am subject to this sudden transformation.[25]

We could come back to the initial point of Sartre that consciousness cannot know itself reflectively but as it can know the world it can know itself similarly that it can know it as an object. The objective state of subjectivity becomes apparent in the effort to know it. Though the emotional state of the subject that Rocquentin is changing but it occurs on the failure to recognise some other person. It seems that actually it is a failure to perform on the objective world.

> ... I tried to pick up a paper lying on the ground and did not succeed - it made a profound impression on me: it occurred to me that I was no longer flee.[26]

Thus Sartre finds subjective state like 'nausea' to occur in an objective world. When Patronne's cousin Adolphe appeared to be nauseating to Rocquentin, he found it in the objective world of the bar only.

> His cotton shirt stands out cheerfully against a chocolate-coloured wall. That too brings on the Nausea The nausea isn't 'inside me : I can feel it over there on the wall ... It is one with cafe, it is I who am inside it.[27]

It shows how reflection of consciousness is made impossible in Sartre's philosophy. This contention of Sartre becomes stronger when Sartre shows how a change in outer world brings a change in subjective state of man. After listening to jazz dominated music in repeating manner when in gramophone Rocquentin heard his most favourite and awaited song "some of these days you will miss me honey" he noticed that his nausea was vanished.

> When the voice sounded in silence, I felt my body hardened and nausea vanished— It filled the room with its metallic transparency crustling our wretched time against the walls, I am in the music.[28]

Adolphe who was in the centre of the world which caused nausea in Rocquentin, becomes a source of happiness.

> Adolphe's face was there set against the chocolate-coloured wall: l press my fingers against the glass, I look at the Adolphe: I am happy.[29]

It seems that it is the 'negation' ascribed by Rocquentin to the walls of the bar, Adolphe etc. Since they do not fulfill the expectation of Rocquentin and caused Nausea in him. In nausea we find the negation of negation and the non-duality of subjectivity and objectivity. It is the non-fulfillment of the subject's expectation from the objective world. Thus 'nothingness' is brought into the world through nausea etc.

But we cannot ignore the subjective aspect of 'nothingness'. Expectation is after all a subjective state of human reality and 'nothingness' is apprehended by man only.

> ... nothingness was just an idea in my head, an existing idea floating in that immensity: This nothingness hadn't come *before* existence, — I shouted 'what a filth what a filth' and shook myself to get lid of this sticky dirt, but it held fast and there was so much of it, tons and tons of existence, indefinitely I was suffocating at the bottom of that huge boredom. And then all of a sudden, the park emptied as if through a big hole the world disappeared. I could not see it any more : there remains some yellow earth around me....[30]

Though 'nothingness' is an idea but existence is prior to that idea. We have discussed so far that out of the non-fulfillment of the expectation to restore the 'lack' man brings 'nothingness'. But the full positive 'existence' cannot cause this non-fulfillment. From Sartre's discussion it seems that 'nothingness' can only appear on the fullness of the existence. But it can only be apprehended by man. Thus in sight of the park we find Rocquentin to see a 'conspiratorial air' which can bring 'nothingness' over there in the park but through Rocquentin only.

> I had already noticed in things a conspirator air. Was it to me that it was addressed? I regretfully felt that I had no means of understanding — I could not understand it even if stayed leaning against the gate hundred and seven years: I had learned everything I could know about existence.[31]

Here Sartre sounds similar to Husserl that it is the transcendental consciousness only can know the world essentially. Husserl's "phenomenological reduction" would then be acceptable by Sartre. But we should not be oblivious of the importance Sartre has given to the existential world.

> Existence is not something which allows itself to be thought of from a distance: it has to invade you, huge motionless animal— existence everywhere to infinity – superfluous always and everywhere: in order to imagine nothingness you had to be there already light in the world.[32]

This shows how subjectivity and objectivity ale fused into one another in human experience. 'Nothingness' indicates a human reality which can only be conceived by men but it appears in the world.

Nothingness–A Fusion of Possibility and Impossibility

The world cannot always fulfill the expectation of man. Thus 'nothingness' in its social connotation seems to be expressing the dual appearance of the world as both 'possibility' and 'impossibility. We will see how social 'possibility' creates lack in man and becomes an impossibility. No duality is considered by Sartre between 'possibility' and 'impossibility' when the very 'possibility of man becomes an 'impossibility' for him he brings a 'nothingness' into the world.

> Every man is defined negatively by the sum total of the possible which are impossible for him: that is by a future more or less blocked off.[33]

For Example, 'medicine' is a social 'possibility' but an 'impossibility' for those who cannot afford to study medicine, thus a 'nothingness' is brought into the world. This individual consciousness of 'nothingness' can lead to a social possibility. So 'nothingness' is not negation which man ascribes to the world out of the non-fulfillment of his expectation. 'Nothingness' at the same time indicates, both consideration of 'lack' in the subject in relation to the world which appears as a 'possibility' but "blocked off" for him and the drive which he can take to surpass the 'impossibility' and create another 'possibility' in the world. If we have to define "nothingness" with the help of social connotation of it, we can say that first it is the human behaviour that ascribes possibility and impossibility to the world and drives for another possibility. Thus 'nothingness' appears to be a reconciliation of subjectivity and objectivity of human reality. We can discuss the matter with the help of an example cited by Sartre. A 'black man' who is potential to be 'pilot' is prohibited from being a crew member by the British colonialism. Here the being of the 'pilot' which is a social possibility appears 'impossibility' for the 'black man'. For this prohibition he finds 'lack' in him and tries to surpass the 'lack' of the objective situation or the social situation; so he flew a plane over to France and was killed over there which results into a revolt from the "black community" against British racism. Though the air-plane thief provoked revolt, he is no more in that revolt. Not because he dies but in every walk of life we can witness that result of our actions supersede us. We can see how man is always objectified in his own creation". First, world and its systems objectifies man, then man's own creation objectifies him.

World as an Objectification of Man

We find Sartre describing the system of a country which every man is facing everywhere, in some way objectifies man.

> The system is a great external machine which might be called the objective mind of United States — it is a monstrous complex of myth, values, prescriptions, slogans, figures and rites... They struggle against it, they constantly suffer from it or reinvent it, they freely give themselves over to it or struggle furiously to elude it; come what may, it transcends them and stands apart from them, for they are men and it is a thing.[34]

But by struggling against such objectivity, man cannot surpass objectivity for ever. But what man will create, is another objective situation. It seems that though the 'impossibility' is coming as the social prohibition, but since

Sartre believes in freedom no condition can reduce human reality into inaction. He does not find any objective situation to be a condition to take man away from his subjectivity.

> Thus the subjectivity contains within itself the objective which it denies and which it surpasses to new objectivity; and this new objectivity by virtue of *objectification* externalises the internality of the project as an objectified subjectivity. This means both that the lived as such finds its place in the result and the projected meaning of the action appears in the reality of the world that it may get its truth in the process of totalisation.[35]

The subject always surpasses the objective situation in which it is present and goes towards the new objective situation which he tries to have. The new objective situation may not keep the expectation of the subject since as an outcome or result it actually expresses not only the subjectivity of a single man but "men in plural" surpasses the individuality. It is called by Sartre as 'counter finality' since the finality or the result of man's action instead of fulfilling his expectation counter him in return. This very objectivity expresses man's situation in the world. It expresses the situation of the whole human race, so it seems to be the 'totality' of man but his totality is actually the 'totalisation'. For the on-going nature of human action no 'totality' is conceivable. Any human action will express the 'dialectic' between man and the world that is the 'dialectic' between 'totality' and 'totalisation'.

Sartre discusses the critical experience of totalising movement which for him cannot be the conception of the movement but a participation in that movement. Sartre finds such experience to be "reflective experience". By 'reflection' Sartre does not mean that consciousness is grasped in singularity of its moments distinguishable from totalisation. But it seems that for Sartre it is 'totalisation' in which human praxis is always engaged with "singular adventure" in a "singular condition".

For Sartre the destiny before human praxis is to achieve the 'totality' but man's singular action cannot determine the 'totality' but keep it as a process of 'totalisation'. The universality of human praxis consists in its being a singular adventure for ever. Universality of human action expresses the totality of human action as a process of singular action.

> ... primacy characteristics of critical experience – goes on inside the totalisation, and cannot be contemplative grasp of the tatalising movement; this means the critical experience can be and should be the reflective experience of any one at all – Indeed when I say that the experience must be reflective, I mean that it is no more distinguishable in the singularity of its moments from the totalisation in process than the reflection is distinguishable from the human praxis... If the totalisation is in process in any sector – can only be singular adventure under singular condition, and it produces universals which illuminates it... Thus the universals of the dialectic – its principles and its laws of intelligibility – are singularised universals.[36]

On going singular actions of man do not allow the 'totality' of human praxis to be a static one. No considerable duality between 'totality' and the 'totalisation' seems to exists thereby. We can consider 'totality' as the 'objectivity' of human praxis as we have already discussed how individual human action is objectified in the world as it is lost in the world as it is lost in the action of "men in plural". Thus no duality between subjective human action and the objectivity of human action remains there. We can say that every subjective action keeps the objectivity of human action as a process of objectification. Thus out of this objectification or totalisation, no generality of human action should be conceived.

Human Reality: A Dialectic between Totality and Totalisation

Consequently, this 'toialisation' or objectification cannot

be experienced from being outside the process. The critical experience as proposed by Sartre to grasp the process of totalisation is described by him as 'Apodectic experience' which implies an experience by participating in the process, not of course by bracketing it. The 'dialectic' between 'totality' and 'totalisation' that is the 'dialectic' between subjectivity of human action and the objectivity of human action cannot be experienced from a subjective point of view. It has to be experienced as being participated in the totalisation process.

> .... Dialectical reason has to be grasped initially through human relation, then its fundamental characteristics imply that it appears as apodectic experience in its very intelligibility.[37]

'Apodectic experience' does not indicate any transcendental experience since it can be had only in the concrete existential world".[38]

> "It is necessary to find our apodectic experience in the concrete world of history.

As for Sartre, human action cannot be derived from any generality of human action, the concrete history cannot be taken as prior condition for human action. Here Sartre differs from Marxists. Marxists consider men to make their own history in a given circumstance, whereas for Sartre, men make their own history by surpassing the given circumstances.

> "The feature of dialectical materialism contained in the statement of Marx "Men make their own history.... but under circumstances ... given and transmitted by the past". But ... the dialectical rationality, the whole of which is contained in this sentence, must be seen as permanent and dialectical unity of freedom and necessity.[39]

Here particular individual actions seem to be the necessary outcome of the 'totality' of human situation for

Marx. Sartre opposes the idea of considering socio-political as the 'antecedent' of man's action. He cannot consider the socio-political world as something like a prior condition of human action rather he believes in the "freedom" of human. He believes it whatever be the socio-political situation, it is made up of man's unconditioned choice of action and if man finds it to supersede him, it is due to the fact that "Others" are equally exercising their freedom in making the world as this or that. Like most of the hermeneutic philosophers, Sartre does not neglect concrete individual action.

"If one tried to see in avarice of a particular group or person only, the simple result of economic Malthusianism, one would fail to discover the concrete reality. For avarice stems from the earliest years of childhood when the child scarcely know what money is.[40]

Sartre suggests not to deduce concrete from general. But for him all concrete incidents should be studied in the context of a social system.

> "... it is impossible to deduce the concrete from general or to dissolve the concrete into general. The connect procedure is to study this concrete characteristics against the background of the economic movement but without misunderstanding their specific nature".[41]

We can interpret Sartre's philosophy to be rooted in the socio-political situation of the then society. Though Sartre does not believe that individual action is deducible from any socio-political system, he suggests the study of individual action should occur against the background of socio-economic movement. We should try to differentiate between the intention of Sartre in considering something as a background and something as a generality. In this regard we should not be oblivious of the fact of the freedom of individual action. If a man chooses for 'avarice' it may be caused by the economic condition of his country where money is scarce or may be the accumulation of money is a mark of social status. But this does not mean that it is an expression of

Malthusianism which is actually the ideology of capitalists to accumulate lots of money without allowing it to circulate. The socio-economic situation can be considered as to form a background which is different from conceiving any socio-political situation to be the generality of any individual action. If we do not differentiate, we will fall into the error of reducing every individual avarice in-to the generality of capitalism. 'Totalisation' is a "multidimensional unity" of individual action.[42]

He thinks that the error we commit by going from particular to general, could be avoided by having an understanding of human action as to pass from 'simple' to 'complex' action in the world. For Sartre, the significance of collective actions narrows down the universality or the generality of human action.

> "... the concrete and lived history gives birth to particular system of ideas -- charged with new significations; their universal meaning is narrowed and deepened. Thus the general categories of culture – which express them, are already objectification of a class, the reflection of conflicts – and particular manifestation of alienation.[43]

Thus it seems that the world despite being made up of human action, expresses 'objectification' or 'alienation' in terms of conflict between man and the world. Sartre's concept of 'emotion' which is to change the world as discussed in ch. II rises from a conflict in the world.

> "... whatever an ideological project may be in appearance, its ultimate goal is to change the basic situation by becoming aware of its contradiction sprung from a particular conflict which expresses the universality of class condition."

We can say that in this way man finds the world to be 'difficult' and he tries to change it.

We have tried to arrive at a socio-political moorings of Sartre's concept or 'nothingness' which is brought into the world by men. The drive of men out of his negative situation can have a hermeneutical interpretation. We can point out how Sartre's idea of 'nothingness' is actually rooted in some socio-political context. The social 'possibility' brings an 'impoverishment' or 'lack' in man that takes him out of that situation, but the result he gets by his going out, objectifies him. Since, it is a situation which cannot be 'dissolved' into the subjective action, and the apparent duality between subjective action and objective outcome can be reconciled only by considering subjective actions as pertaining to the social-historical world. The socio historical world of post war situation which appears to be really difficult to man, as it appears in all respects as an impossibility to man, thus 'impoverishment' or 'lack' is the subjectivity for man. It seems that in this period there is no way to look into man's inside, since, man is found always with his drive for attaining something. His concept of history as being made of individual's action and irreducible to individual action shows Sartre's effort to reconcile between subjectivity and objectivity. These methods are similar to that of hermeneutics. The 'objectivity' of the world which actually means the absence of the fulfillment of expectation is designed by man's individual action. It does not indicate any generality of man's action. If the world is the source of the 'impoverishment' it is made by man's action – man's 'subjectivity' by creating a 'possibility' for some people and creating 'impossibility' for some other people. But as man finds the world to be 'difficult' he has the emotion to change the world.

So far as the being of the 'fundamental project' is concerned, that is the being of the 'causa-sui' the 'self-cause' which is expressed in all 'particular projects', it is a hermeneutical effort of Sartre. Every expression is considered as the expression of that which is expressed (discussed in chapter IV). We must mention here that for Sartre, actions are not the symbol or expression of 'totality' and we should avoid using the hermeneutical word 'expression' for 'particular project'. In hermeneutical philosophy this kind of interpretation indicates author's socio-political background or situation which has been expressed through the writing of the author. For every text, a hermeneutic philosopher tries to trace out the socio-political background which is actually expressed through author's thought. By taking a hermeneutical stand point with respect to Sartre we can see how Sartre's writing are rooted in some socio-historical context and Sartre himself is taking a hermeneutical stand-point when he interprets every human action as rooted in a socio-historical situation. It will also bring out Sartre's effort to show the socio-historical world as reconciliation between subjective action and objective outcome of it. By using such hermeneutical method, it would be difficult to show how every subjective action can manifest the 'fundamental project' to be the God of his being. By tracing out the socio-political background of Sartre's thought, we can only bring out the cause for Sartre's concept of man as with the despair for ever which persuades him to act throughout his life without a break and characterise man as 'nothing' in itself. But we cannot bring out from any socio-political activity of man that it is the expression of that 'fundamental project' which indicates an abstract goal. Godhood is definitely an abstract goal. It is possible to interpret only with the method of "a priori description" of 'particular project', as a manifestation of, fundamental project', 'causa-sui'. But then the objection raised by Sartre against Husserl as discussed in chapter II cannot be sustained. Sartre also will commit the error of believing in essential cognition about man in terms of 'fundamental project'. Consequently, it would be meaningless to talk of the freedom of the 'particular project'.

The concept of 'fundamental project' could have been avoided by Sartre, but it seems that he cannot describe human reality as 'nothingness' without the support of it that is without making the ultimate or the fundamental aspiration of man as unattainable. We should notice the change in his position Sartre has made in his later writing. In his earlier works he emphasised on the similarity of the nature of being with God for which man aspires. It is due to paradoxical desire of man to possess freedom and at the same time to flee from it in order to escape ceaseless action. Man expresses his paradoxical desire to assert his subjectivity through his action and at the same time to be objectified to get rid of action. But in Sartre's later writings, we find men with the tireless effort to protect his subjectivity from all around objectification. God which indicates a subject-object unity remains as an abstract goal in comparison to the concrete goal of man's life, that is the goal of 'particular project, gets less importance in Sartre's later writings though he did not discard the abstract goal. But felt the need of its concretisation.

> Abstract intentions should not exist in isolation and sent out into the void appeals which have no direct influence on human condition….ideal goal should be transformed into immediate material goals.

Sartre seems to feel the necessity of the abstract goal to be interpreted from objective stand-point of individual. The goals for which man aspires, is to get his expectations fulfilled in spite of the 'objectification' of him in the world of 'other'. To achieve this goal man has to struggle for his whole life without being successful. Success cannot come to him due to the existence of freedom of 'Other'. Actually it is human freedom which is in struggle. A profound understanding of human reality of Sartre makes this kind of interpretation of man possible. This understanding cannot be an out come of an experience confined to certain place or certain time.

Hermeneutical experience which has a socio-political mooring of certain place and certain time cannot be the experience with which Sartre is dealing. Sartre's experience can only be understood as an intuitive experience. He experiences the concrete human behaviour and intuits a 'fundamental' behaviour out of that experience.

References

1. Mill, J.S., *System of Logic Book* III. Ch. I. Ed. People New Impression, Longman Green and Company 39, Paternoster 1961, p. 283.
2. CDRI, p 35.
3. *Bhadra M. K. A Critical Study of Sartre's Ontology of Consciousness,* pp. 37-39.
4. *Ibid.,* p. 9.
5. Page C. Philosophical hermeneutics and its meaning for philosophy. *Philosophy Today* Vol. 35. No. 2/4 Summer 91. p. 128.
6. K. Muller, Vollmer. *The Hermeneutic Reader*, p. 122.
7. BN., p. 303.
8. BN., p. 303.
9. BN., pp. 349-353.
10. BN., p. 360.
11. p. 93, PM.
12. PM., p. 91.
13. PM., pp. 79-88.
14. *Ibid.,* p. 80.
15. CDR I., p. 349.
16. Benichon P., Interview with Sartre. Trans P. Southgate Esquire 78 (Dec. '72) p. 13.
17. CDR I., p. 130.
18. CDR I., p. 123.
19. CDR I., p. 113.
20. BN., pp. 42-43.
21. BN., p. 58.
22. Nausea, p. 9.
23. Nausea, p. 10.
24. *Ibid.,* p. 13.

26\. Nausea, p. 20.

25\. *Ibid.,* pp. 13-14.

27. Nausea, p. 37.
28. *Ibid.*, p. 38.
29. Nausea, pp. 38-39.
30. *Ibid.*, p. 193.
31. Nausea, p. 193.
32. *Ibid.*, p. 190-193.
33. PM., p. 95.
34. PM., p. 98.
35. PM., p. 98.
36. CDR I., p. 44.
37. *Ibid.*, p. 35.
38. *Ibid.*, p. 75.
39. PM., p. 102.
40. PM., pp. 102-103.
41. PM., p. 111.
42. PM., pp. 112-13.
43. Situation II, p. 293.

Conclusion

In Sartre's philosophy we find that man stands for subjectivity and the world of 'others' stands for objectivity. Consciousness as a non-substantial subjectivity is for ever separated from the substantial world but remains as the only source of the revelation of the substantial world. Similarly, man as a subjectivity, is for ever alienated from the world which is revealed as this or that through the action of man only. This revelation is continuous and ceaseless because if we take a single man out of the world and try to see the process of revelation through his action, we will find the world as a whirlpool on which every human action is like a drop of water which vanishes every time. Man is with the ceaseless possibility whereas world is an impossibility for him. But the being of the man consists in surpassing the impossibility infinitely. Sartre is not bracketing the world like Husserl as a source of infinity. Rather, for Sartre, world is the source of 'objectification' as well as a source of infinity and in order to surpass objectification man too becomes the source of the infinity of his action. Man tries to assert his action repeatedly in the world which has been lost in the milieu of the world. Thus Sartre's method is not Husserlian. In Husserlian method the question of surpassing does not arise since the world is bracketed. Sartre finds phenomenology, an "escapist's doctrine". Moreover, if the world is bracketed and the only source of understanding is the cognition of essential knowledge about the world by the transcendental consciousness, we could call Husserl's method a subjective method. Sartre on the other hand, bases the understanding of human reality on both world and individual man. Though, world is the source of 'objectification, it is actually a conglomeration of subjective action of 'men in plural'.

Heidegger's method begins as an objective method. Being for him is self revealing, appears as a general context of the relation between man and the world. But when understanding of the being is concerned, Heidegger expresses his belief in 'authentic' understanding of the world or being. This cannot be acquired by taking general view on the world but a subjective view on it. While explaining the being, Heidegger took an objective point of view and while interpreting human understanding, he took a subjective stand point. The phenomenological method of Sartre's predecessors cannot be a reconciliation of subjectivity and objectivity, which is the main characteristic of Sartre's method.

We find a reconciliation of subjective action with its objective outcome in Sartre's philosophy, as the latter is formed by the former. This effort reconciles the particular human action with the universal of world's human action as the former is expressing the latter. But the particular human action cannot be derived from any universal or general nature of human action. Particular actions are designing the universal but not the other way round. Thus, Sartre's method may have some similarities with induction. But Sartre does not consider any gulf between particular project and universal from the particular. The universal gets expressed only through particulars. Thus the sphere of universality is narrowed down. Sartre believes that only by a priori description a 'particular project' of man can be judged as a manifestation of the 'fundamental project' which he gives a universal connotation. But as a priori description is not experiential description, Sartre could not have any right to criticise Husserl as to give an escapist's doctrine. Sartre cannot escape the experiential world. Rather, he has to refute the possibility of knowing the world essentially because both the world and man are in a relation which is a continuous process. The experiential world is the only platform for Sartre to understand human reality. The platform is the socio-political world.

This socio-political context is the aim of hermeneutic philosophers which they try to trace behind every text of authors. This socio-political context can also be brought out of Sartre's writing. Along with it, we can find Sartre's hermeneutical effort to interpret human behaviour in the socio-political context. There is some similarity between the method of Sartre and that of hermeneutic philosophers regarding the reconciliation between subjectivity and objectivity. Hermeneutic philosophers, although consider history or 'life world' to be made of man's action but not by surpassing the history as Sartre believes. Here Sartre differs from Marx also.

By this constant surpassing man brings 'nothingness' to the world. 'Nothingness' comes in the world as both the present state of man and the world in which man finds himself as nihilated by man. This 'nothingness' is not caused by man himself but man experiences nothingness. For Sartre 'Nothingness' is not a 'transcendental' understanding of the world by man. Rather it is the spatio-temporal evanescent world made by "men in plural" with it's multidimensional structure which supersede individual human expectation. Man directs himself outside to negate its present state and thereby the present world but due to the non-fulfillment of his expectation he has to negate the outside world again and thus man brings 'nothingness' into the world. It brings an anguish in man. Man cannot withdraw himself from action. He can experience that he has the freedom to act but no freedom not to act. Man's freedom makes him responsible for the whole world along with 'others'. He finds himself thrown into this world of action as he is not responsible for his reducibility to action. But man tries to get the hold over his being, he likes to enjoy freedom and at the same time not to be reduced to action. For Sartre man's freedom indicates nothing but his reducibility to action. Thus man's aspiration indicates a conflict between his action and his aspiration. The moment man will have a hold over his being or becomes the cause of his being what is called 'causa-sui', the being which is similar, to God, he will not allow himself to be reduced to action. Thomas C. Anderson has made a wonderful remark in this regard, he holds that man's action and aspiration does not express 'antagonism' if it does not pursue to become God.[1]

But we find many experiential aspects in Sartre's philosophy, for considering God as the goal of human aspiration. Where as God whom we pray and God we try to be, are conceived on the basis of the experience of limitation of our being. In case of prayer, we know that we have freedom but we experience the limitation in shaping our life or fulfilling our desire. In case of aspiration, to be God, we try to flee from our freedom and try to have a being which has freedom but not reduced to action. Our experiences show our freedom as threatened by 'Other's' freedom and wishes to have a hold over all men and all work and to become a God.

With the profound experience of human condition that man is nothing but outward drive from himself and the world which does not fulfill his expectation, Sartre has conceived man as 'nothingness'. James Edie rightly interprets that Sartrean freedom consists in the "experiential ability of consciousness" to stand back from itself as not-substantial absolute.[2] Man experiences that man could participate as well observed his being lost in the world.

According to T. C. Anderson Sartre denies the possibility of man to have a subject to subject relationship with others. For Anderson, Sartre considers experience of sympathetic situation a psychological experience not ontological. Ontological or actual relation among men is subject-object relation. For T. C. Anderson, Sartre considers the experience of subject-object relation a lateral awareness not a direct experience. But we should remember that Sartre denies "contemplative grasp" of totality. How can he accept contemplative grasp of subject-object relation without having a direct experience. Anderson finds Sartre neglecting the possibility of gentle or caring 'Look' by other. Thus he finds Sartre's concept of human relation as an abstract concept which he overcomes in his Notebooks. According to Anderson, Sartre overcomes in *Notebooks* the abstract concept of freedom consisting in unbound-unpredictable human action – appeared in his earlier writing. In Notebooks Sartre accepts economic and technological limits of human action which Anderson finds as Sartre's acceptance of subject to subject relation. But Sartre should not be criticised on this ground. If he would uphold an abstract concept of absolute freedom, he could not consider subject, object relation as the only relation among men as he had to consider other's freedom too. Anderson seems to overlook Sartre's idea of 'general' ground of objectification where both 'I' and 'thou' are objectified. If Sartre is talking about subject-object relation it is between man and the world. Not between I and thou. 'I' and 'thou' are in a circularity of objectification where both are objectified as a complementary to another's subjectivity.

Sartre's interpretation of man's subjectivity as the source of all 'objectivity' or his being lost in the world seems to be rooted in the experience of Sartre of the post war socio-political situation. This period was not a time for self knowledge rather man is always found with a push towards the world and being pushed out by the world. The then society which was marked by scarcity, deprivation, discrimination, violence and revolution seems to have influenced Sartre to find the world both as possibility and impossibility. It is due to his experience of the post war situation, he finds it responsible to create 'lack' in man in terms of prohibition etc.

Despite having the moorings of post-war period, Sartre's philosophy can be said to have a universality. Every singular activity is interpreted by Sartre as the manifestation of the totality. The existence of violence all over the world seems to make Sartre convinced that a man who is taking part in any violent activity directly or indirectly is manifesting the totality of violence. Though Sartre's philosophy seems to be originated from the post war situation of East-European country, his philosophy is representing a view applicable to any time and any socio-political world. His philosophy appears to be a reconciliation between singular subjective action and global objective action.

From the above discussion it is clear that Sartre's philosophical method can be described as experiential. The socio- historical world of post-war situation has a deterministic role in Sartre's philosophical thought. But right from the explanation of consciousness to the objectification of man in the world Sartre's thought indicates his profound intuitive ability to describe human reality as a whole. Giving maximum importance to the particular action of man he finds men, objectified in the world. Sartre's experience of socio-historical world, being coupled with his philosophical insight, has been able to conceive human reality to uphold the truth for all time and places.

References

1. Anderson, T.C., "Antagonism in Sartre's Philosophy, International", *Philosophical Quarterly,* Vol. 29, No. 2, Issue No. 114, June 1989, p. 140.
2. Edie James, M., "The Question of Transcendental Ego", Sartre's critique of Husserl, *Journal of British Society for Phenomenology,* Vol. 24, No. 2, May 1993, p. 111.

Bibliography

PRIMARY SOURCE

Baudelaire: Trans Martin turnel? : Hamish Hamilton, London 1953.

Being and Nothingness: A Phenomenological Essay on Ontology. Trans. with an Intro. H.E. Barners, University of Colorado: Washington Square Press Pocket Books, U.S.A. 1966.

Between Existentialism and Marxisim : Trns John Mathews : Willim Marrow and Company, New York 1974.

Critique of Dialectical Reason. Vol. I : Theory of Practical Ensemble, Trans. Allan Sheridon : New Left Books, London. 1976.

Critique of Dialectical Reason. Vol. II (Unfinished). The Intelligibility of History. Ed. By Arlette Elkaim Sartre, Trans. Quintin Hoar : Verso, London, New York, 1991.

Emotion Outline of a Theory: Trans. Barnerd Freehtman : The Wisdom, Library, New York, 1948.

Essay in Aesthetics: Selected and Trans. Wade Baskin : Peter Queen, London, 1963.

Existentialism and Humanism: Trans. with Intro Philip Mariet: Mathuen and Company Ltd., London, 1948.

Iron in the Soul. Intro. David Caute : Penguin. Modern Classics.

Life/Situations : Pantheon Books, New York, Trans. Random House Inc., 1977.

Materialism and Revolution : Tans. Forest William and Robert Kirkpatrik : The Noonday Press, New York, 1957.

Nausea. Trans. Robert Baldick, Penguin Books.

Notebooks for an Ethic : Trans. David Pellauer; University of Chicago Press, Chicago and London, 1992.

Prychology of Imagination. Trans. B Freehtman : Mathuen and Company Ltd., London, 1872.

Saint, Gnet, Actor and Martyr W.H. Allen, London, 1963.

Situation I, Literary and Philosophical Essay : Philoshophical Library. Gallimard, 1957.

Situation II, What is Literature? Philosophical Library. 1947.

Situation III, Literary and Philosophical Essay : Philosophical Library, Gallimard, 1957.

The Age of Reason : Trans. Eric Shutton : Hamish Hamilton London, 1947.

The Problem of Method : Trans. with Intro. by Hazel E. Barnes: Mathuen and Company Ltd., London, 1963.

The Reprieve: Trans. Eric Shutton. Intro. David Cante : Penguin Books in Assoc. with Hamish Hamilton.

The Wall and Other Short Stories: Trans. Liyod Alexander, New York, New Direction, 1969.

The Words: Trans. Rene Clephona : Penguin Books in Assoc. with Hamish Hamilton, 1987.

Transcendence of the Ego: Trans. Forest Williams and Robert Kirkpatrik : The Noonday Press, New York, 1957

What is Literature. Trans B. Frechtman. Mathuen and Company Ltd., London., 1978.

WORKS OF OTHERS

Deflem Mathuein (Ed.), Habermas, *Law and Modernity* : Sage Publication, 1998.

Husserl Edmund, The Train of Thoughts in the Lectures: From April 26 to May 2, 1950, Nakhikian, 1969.

Muller – Vollmer K. (Ed.), The Hermeneutic Reader: Text of the German Tradition from the Endightenment the Present, Basil Blackwell, U.K., 1985.

Ricoeur Paul, History and Truth: Trans. With Intro Charles A. Kelbly : North Western University Press, Evanston, 1965.

OTHER BOOKS

Anderson Thomac. C. Sartres. Two Ethics: (From Autheuticity to Integral Humanity) : Open Court, Chicago and La Salle, Illinois, 1993.

Barne H.E., Sartre : Quartret Books, London, 1974.

Bhadra M.K., A Critical Study of Sartre's Ontology of Consciousness : The University of Burdwan, 1978.

Bhadra M.K., A Critical Survey of Phenomenology and Existentialism : Indian Council of Philosophical Research, Allied Publisher, New Delhi, 1990.

Bleieher Joseph, Contemporary Hermenentics : Routledge & Kegan Paul, London and New York, 1980.

Cumming R.D. (Ed.), Philosophy of Jean Paul Sartre : Matheuen and Company Ltd., 1988.

Dibadj Sayed Musa, The Authenticity of the Text in Hermeneutics: Qom Iran : The Council for Research of Values and Philo ophy.

Dutta D.M., The Chief Currents of Contemporary Philosophy: The University of Calcutta.

Flynn Thomas R., Sartre and Narxist Existentionlism : The University of Cicago Press, Cicago and London.

Guignon Charles B., Cambridge Companion to Heidgger : Cambridge University Press 1993.

Hodges H.A. William Dilthey, An Introduction : Routledge & Kegan Paul, 1949.

I Lowels Christina, Cambridge Companion to Sartre : Cambridge University Press, 1993.

Laing R.D. and Coope D.G., Reason and Violence : A Decade of Sartre's Philosophy 1950-60, Tavistock Publications, London, 1964.

Lichtheim George, The Concept of Ideology and other Essay : Vintage Books, A Division of Random House, New York, 1967.

Marrill Alberes Rene, Jean Paul, Sartre, A Philosopher without Faith : The Merline Press, London, 1961-1964.

Murdoch Irish, Sartre, Romantic Rationalist : Fountana Library, Bowes and Bowes Ltd.

Olson Robert G., An Introduction to Existentialism : Dover Publication Inc., New York, 1962.

Schrader George Alfred (Jr.), Existential Philosophers Kierkegaard to Merlean Ponty: McGraw-Hill Company, New York, 1967.

Smith Borry and Smith Woodstuff (Ed.), The Cambridge Companion To Husserl : Cambridge University Press, 1995.

Solomon R.C., Continental Philosophy Since 1750 : The Rise and Fall of the Self : Oxford University Press, Oxford, New York, 1988.

Thevenaz Pierre, What is Phenomenology ? Ed. and Intro. James Edie : Quadrangle Books Inc., Cicago, 1962.

Vattimo Geanni, Beyond Interpretation : The meaning of Hermeneutic Philosophy, Trans. David Webb : Polity Press, 1997.

Warnock Mary, Existantialism : Oxford University Press, 1970.

White Stephen K. (Ed.), The Cambridge Companion to Habermas: Cambridge University Press, 1995.

JOURNALS

Agarwal, M.M., "Nothingness and Freedom : Sartre and Krishnamisti. *Journal of Indian Council of Philosophical Research* : Vol. IX, No. Sep. to Dec. '91.

Antomy M., "The Non-being of Nothingness". *Journal of British Society for Phenomenology* : Vol. 19. Jan. '88. pp. 90-92.

Anderson T.C., "Antagonism in Sartre's Philosophy", *International Philosophical Quarterly*: Vol. 29, No. 114, June 89, pp. 140-149.

Blosser P., "The a Prior in Phenomenology and Legacy of Logical Empiricism". *Philosophy Today*: Vol. 4, No. 2/4, Summer '97, pp. 195-200.

Bruce, B., "Antagonism in Sartre's Being and Nothingness" *History of European Ideas* : Vol. 22. No. 33, May 96. pp. 193-215.

Edie James, M., "The Question of Transcendental Ego : Sartre's Critique of Husserl", *Journal of British Society for Phenomenology*: Vol 24. No. 2, May 93, pp. 5-9.

Gregory, M., "Sartre between Realism and Idealism", *Philosophy Today*: Vol. I. No. 2, Summer '93, pp. 286-307.

Jopling, David, "Sartre the long distance Truck Driver". *Journal of British Society for Phenemenology*: Vol. 24. No. 3, Oct. '93, pp. 9-37.

Michal, H., "Bad Faith" Philosophy: Vol. 64, July '89, pp. 397-462.

NIyen, A.T., "Hermenential Understanding A defence of History *Journal of Thought*: Vol. 29. No. 2, Summer 94, pp. 19-32.

Page, Carl, "Philosophical Hermeneutics and Its Meaning for Philosophy', *Philosophy Today*: Vol. 35. No. 2/4, Summer '91, pp. 127-130.

Robert, B., "The Prospect of Community in Later Sartre", *International Philosophical Quarterly*: Vol 29. Jan. 89, pp. 139-149.

Roy, Krishna, "Man and Hermencutics", *Journal of ICPR* : Vol. VII. No. 3, May to August 1990, pp. 12-20.

Sing, R.M. "Is there abrak in Sartre's Thought", *International Philosophical Quarterly*, Vol. 21. No. 4, Oct. '94, pp. 279-285.

Steven, B.L. "Nothingness and Sartre's Fundamental Project" *Philosophy Today* : Vol 38. No. 2, Summer '94, pp. 191-203.

Sutton, M.P. "Sartre on self Deceiver Transcendent Consciousness", *Journal of British Society for Phenomenology*: Vol. 23. No. 2, Oct. '92, pp. 103-119.

Sutton, M.P., "Sartre on Temporality". *Journal of British Society for Phenomenology*: Vol. 20. Jan. '89, pp. 23-32.

William, Irwin, "Sartre on Emotion." Dialogue PST: Vol. 38. No. 1, Oct. '95, pp. 1-7.

Index